Tarot Inte

By Paul Foster Case

and Wade Coleman

Edited by Wade Coleman

Forward

Tarot Interpretations concludes Paul Foster Case's Tarot lesson series. My intention in editing Case's masterpieces is to make the lessons easier to understand for the modern reader.

If you are interested in reading Case's original Tarot text, they can be found on Amazon. The first lesson, *An Introduction to the Tarot* is published as *The Tarot: A Key to the Wisdom of the Ages*. The second, *Tarot Fundamentals* is retitled *Tarot Card Meanings: Fundamentals*. And the third book, *Tarot Interpretations* is published as *Tarot Revelations*.

Table of Content

TAROT INTERPRETATION

Chapter 1

The Hidden Force

You have completed your preliminary study of the Tarot. Now you will learn how to use the Tarot Keys to realize your heart's desire.

We assume that your heart's desire involves no conflict with the rights and happiness of others. Nothing in occultism will enable you to gain any tricky advantage over another human being. Your previous studies have taught you the folly of expecting something for nothing. It is impossible to employ the higher forces for anything but right ends.

All a black magician accomplishes is their downfall, their own mental and physical deterioration. Selfish personal motives are enough to debar anyone from making use of subtle spiritual energy. Selfishness clouds the mind so that it cannot perceive the significance of the instruction.

However clear the teaching, they who would misuse it is sure to misunderstand it.

The ignorant cannot employ powers reserved for the expression of wisdom. Study and practice as much as they may, those who intend to use Ageless Wisdom to further their interests at the expense of another will meet with nothing but disappointment.

Consider your motives. More than anything else, what you want to be? What you want to do? See yourself engaged in the kinds of action appropriate to the expression of your heart's desire. Make your mental images clear and definite. You cannot be too specific.

Vivid imagery includes all the necessary details as to the possession of the means or instrumentalities you may need to carry out your action. Set your mental stage with scenery appropriate to the realization of your desire. To see yourself having what you need is far less important than to see yourself *doing what you want to do.*

Pay no attention to those who say that you only need to hold fast to the essential idea of your primary purpose. It doesn't work. You must have a definite plan or central motive. This is indispensable. To experience full realization, the idea must be clothed with specific mental imagery.

We assume that you know what you want, and you are ready to devote yourself to the realization of your aim. This being understood, fix firmly in mind the fundamental principle of this course of instruction.

Realization is a state of consciousness. It is the illumined perception of things as they are, displacing the deluded acceptance of things as they look.

The twenty-two Tarot Keys are designed to bring about a change of consciousness. They were invented by adepts. They represent the fundamental states of human consciousness. Those who impress these symbols deeply upon their brain cells plants the seeds of illumined realization.

Key 0 pictures the hidden force at work in the process of realization. Your previous studies presented ideas to the meaning of Key 0. The degree of your success in doing what you want to do will be measured by your understanding of its more profound significance. It sums up what the wise learned about the One Energy behind all appearances. It tells you what they do and don't know.

The force which makes possible the realization of your heart's desire is occult because it is hidden from the ignorant. In the dawn of a New Age, more people are ready to assimilate and apply this ancient knowledge; but even today, prepared minds are in the minority. From the minority are chosen the real, though hidden, masters of the world.

The wise do not pretend to know the innermost nature of the hidden force. None pretends to define it. Lao-tze says of it: "The TAO, which is the subject of discussion, is not the true Tao; the quality which can be named is not its true attribute."

Occult names for the hidden force are designations or identifying labels. We do not know what it is, any more than we know what electricity is, and nobody needs to know. The wise avoid useless quest in this direction.

The hidden force is the One Thing, which is the source of everything. It cannot be identified with any of the things which proceed from it. Therefore the hidden force is called the No-Thing.

The zero sign (0) is a symbol of the No-Thing. Zero also signifies freedom from the limitations called *time* and *space*. Therefore The Fool shows the hidden is always at the height of its power. However, there is always something higher beyond. It has limitless possibilities for finer and better types of manifestation. Let this realization sink deep into your mind. *Time and space cannot bind the hidden force. It is always free. No conditions can limit its self-expression.*

Being boundless, it is necessarily omnipresent. "All the power that ever was or will be is here now." Its energy manifested as the light of stars, maintains itself without the loss through millions of light-years, and propagates itself through immense reaches of space. Where anything is, it is; and where nothing seems to be, there it is also.

You are filled with the real presence of the hidden force. All that you are is an assemblage of manifold veils that hide it, and, by hiding it, make it "occult." Your body is made of it. It is the substance of your food and drink, of the air you breathe, of the earth beneath your feet, of all your possessions. This is the One Reality, manifest in all the things you know, and in everything outside your present range of knowledge.

The universe is a vast ocean of vibrating electromagnetic energy. This energy appears as "objects" when its vibrations are within relatively narrow fields perceptible to our senses.

If our sense organs should change a little, we should find ourselves in a new world, full of things unknown to us now. These things exist though we cannot form clear ideas of what they are like.

Matter, as a separate entity, does not exist. Everything in the physical plane emerges from an invisible and immaterial source. It is called light when perceived by our eyes. When it warms our skin, it's heat. Physical objects are bound or standing waves of electromagnetic energy.

"Light is the veil of the Boundless, and all things are from that Light," says the Inner School that invented Tarot. "The Word gave life to everything that was created, and his life brought light to everyone," is the declaration of John 1:4.

The living light is called the *Life-Breath*. This is not a figure of speech. Our atmosphere is made of light. The atoms of its gases are built up of electrons, themselves points of radiant energy. Every electron is a point at which lines of magnetic force converge. Their convergence sets up whirling motion at the electronic point. This whirling motion is represented by the ten yellow wheels on the Fool's dress – The Sephiroth on the Tree of Life.

In proportion to their size, electrons are as far apart as the stars. Thus the active units of energy in the universe, the electrons, are separated by relatively vast expanses of apparently empty space.

Dwell on this idea for a while. It will help you overcome one significant obstacle to realization. It seems that things of the physical plane seem hard and solid to our senses. However, they offer no resistance to the passage of the hidden force. Radio waves pass through solid walls to bring music into your home. About 65 billion neutrinos pass through your fingernail every second. The mass of the Earth is hardly a barrier. There are finer vibrations than these, of which nothing physical can be an obstacle.

As we read in the Emerald Tablet of Hermes: "This is the strong force of all forces, overcoming every subtle and penetrating every solid thing."

Electrons are separated from one another by vast expanses of apparently empty space. However, it is not empty. Space is filled with the Life-Breath. It is everywhere, between things as well as in them.

They may be small as electrons or big as Betelgeuse, but things are limited areas or fields, wherein the occult force takes on physical form. *All things are standing waves in an ocean of light.*

The earth is a wheel driven by solar force. The movements of matter on its surface, including your actions, are transformations of the sun's radiance. Everything pictured in Key 0 is an image of a form of solar energy.

The earth is made of electrons that were once part of the sun's mass — the waves upon the shore. The majestic progress of the Amazon, the bubbling of hillside springs, the fall of every raindrop, these are the watery vestures of solar light and heat.

Every breath drawn by living creatures, every transformation of that breath into sound, expresses the same power. Every prayer and every curse, every word of wisdom and every utterance of folly, is made possible by sunshine. The shrill call of bugles sounding the attack, the solemn music echoing beneath cathedral arches--these are the sunlight's garments of air.

Every fire that burns is a flame lit by the sun. The history of human culture is the story of man's mastery of fire. Almost everything we own has passed through fire or fashioned by machines driven by fire. The energy of fuel is imprisoned sunlight. And what's more wonderful than the slow fire in our bodies, lit before our birth, which, while it burns, is life itself? Mastery of this vital flame is one of the greatest occult secrets to be learned from your present studies. Through the functions of our brain, the fire takes form as thought. Like everything else, our brains are made of light. It changes sunlight into mental imagery.

Your thoughts are the cosmic play of light vibration, which implies a mental quality within these waves of living light. It is the hidden force of life and mind, as well as the root of all physical energies. Thus the Fiery Intelligence is attributed to Key 0 and Aleph.

During this week, memorize the following:

Aleph (א) is numerically 1 and transliterated as A.

The letter-name ALF/ALPh (אלף), Aleph, means Ox or Bull. Its numeral value is 111.

Aleph stands for רוח (RVCh), Ruach, the Life-Breath, and the element of Air.

It is the sign of the Fiery Intelligence.

To it is attributed to the planet Uranus.

It is a symbol of superconsciousness.

Whenever you are beset by appearances of limitation, call up before your mind's eye the picture of the Fool. Absorb its message of absolute freedom. Remember, this is a pictorial suggestion formulated by adepts. Your subconsciousness will accept and act upon it. It is a treatment for realization, carefully worked out by Those Who Know.

It is also a means for mental and spiritual contact with members of the Inner School who have completed the work you are now beginning. Make it an integral part of your flesh and blood by looking at it every day, until every detail of the design is imprinted on your brain.

Chapter 2

True Magic

The Emerald Tablet of Hermes is one of the great classics of Ageless Wisdom. It is ascribed to Hermes Trismegistus, and the Egyptian Master said to be the founder of alchemy and magic.

Who wrote this masterpiece of practical occultism we do not know. The oldest versions are in Latin, though there may have been earlier ones in Greek. Scholars generally agreed that the text originated in the early centuries of the Christian era, not to the literature of ancient Egypt.

1. True, without falsehood, certain and most true.

2. That which is above is from that which is below, and that which is below is from that which is above, for the performance of the miracle of the one thing.

3. All things are from One, by the meditation of One, so all things have their birth from this One thing by adaptation.

4. The Sun is its father, the Moon, its mother. The wind carries it in its belly; the earth is its nurse.

5. It is the father of all perfection and the consummation of the whole world.

6. Its power is integrating, if it is converted into Earth.

7. Thou shall separate the Earth from the Fire, the subtle from the gross, suavely, and with great ingenuity.

8. It ascends from the earth to the heaven, and descends again to the earth, and receives the powers of the superiors and inferiors.

9. By this means you shall have the glory of the whole world

10. and all obscurity shall flee from you.

11. It is the force above all forces, overcomes every subtle, and penetrating every solid thing.

12. So the world was created. From this come all wonderful adaptations, of which this is a manner.

13. Hence I am called Hermes Trismegistus, having the three parts of the philosophy of the whole world. What I have to tell you is complete, concerning the operation of the Sun.

Two thousand years ago, the authors did not put their names to occult treatises. Believing themselves to be inspired by gods, or Masters of Wisdom, they would say, "This is a work of Hermes," to give honor to the source of their illumination. In this practice, there is no taint of deception, nor an intent to invest a book with the authority of a great name. The modest geniuses of that day sought to indicate their indebtedness to the higher powers whence their knowledge was derived.

Various traditions concerning The Emerald Tablet have come down to us. One says the thirteen sentences of this treatise were engraved by Hermes Trismegistus, with a stylus of a diamond, on a single large emerald. At his death, the emerald was hidden in his tomb in the Great Pyramid. Centuries later, Alexander the Great found the stone and gave it to the world.

This is an allegory. Emerald is the stone of Venus. Hermes is Mercury, the personification of human intellect. The diamond is attributed to the Sun. It is the force that carves the emerald tablet. Hermes or Mercury directs the solar force, so it is as sharp as a laser beam. Thus the allegory suggests the text was inscribed on the subconsciousness of the human race (Venus, Key 3).

The Great Pyramid is the tomb of Hermes, and his death refers to the temporary loss of ancient knowledge, which is referred to as the Master's Word in old manuscripts.

Alexander the Great symbolizes the school of philosophy, which flourished at Alexandria and symbolized the revival of the lost ancient knowledge.

Eliphas Levi says the Emerald Tablet of Hermes, contains all magic in a single page. It has thirteen sentences in all. Five are in the first paragraph and eight in the second. Five, the proportional height of the Great Pyramid, if its baseline is eight. Five is the number of adaptation, the pentagram, and Humanity. Eight, the number of rhythm, strength, and mastery. Five and eight are the determining numbers of the Vault of Brother C. R., Founder of the Rosicrucian Order.

Each side of this vault was a rectangle, five feet wide, and eight feet high. These two numbers, together with their sum, 13, and their difference, 3, are keys to great secrets of occultism.

The final sentence of The Emerald Tablet makes clear the nature of the Great Work. "I have completed what I have to tell concerning the Operation of the Sun." On Earth, the sun's radiant energy, by adaptation, is active in all activities.

Therefore is the sun placed high in the heavens behind the Fool. The force the Magician draws from above and directs upon the garden below is the same solar energy. Compare Key 0 with Keys 10 and 21. The sun in Key 0 occupies the same position as the eagle's head in Keys 10 and 21. The eagle is a symbol of Scorpio (♏), which governs the reproductive forces.

Scorpio, corresponding to Key 13, rules the eighth house of death, inheritance, secrets, and occultism. Behind the horrible appearance of death, is the secret force in the Great Work. This is the Astral Light of Eliphas Levi, who says the great magical agent is the force which man multiplies in the reproduction of his species.

We should not suppose that the One Energy is only solar radiance. Astral Light means *light of stars*. Levi says the Astral Light is diffused throughout infinity, the substance of heaven and earth, and the First Matter of the Great Work. Therefore solar radiance is a manifestation of the One Energy.

The uplifted wand in the Magician's right-hand points to the corner. In Keys 10 and 21, it is occupied by the head of a man. This man is a symbol for Aquarius (♒). The force the Magician draws down from superconscious levels is conditioned by his perception of the nature and possibilities of humanity. In this dawning of the Aquarian Age, we are beginning to realize that every human is an embodiment, here and now, of the power which produces and governs the universe.

In astrology, Aquarius rules the eleventh house of the horoscope. It is the house of friends, hopes, desires, and aspirations. As we understand that humanity is "but little lower than God," we shall see that our hopes rest on a firm foundation. Since the One Thing is embodied in every human, we realize that its perfect expression on earth results in an era of universal friendship and brotherhood.

This will supplant the pitifully inadequate "civilization" of the Piscean Age, with its fierce competitions, fear-born wars, and follies of racial and national discrimination and hatred.

Thus, in the garden of the Magician, grow the lilies of the right knowledge. A cross-section of their flowers is a six-pointed star or Shield of David. David (דוד) means *love* or *the beloved*. Thus the Shield of David signifies *the protection of love*.

Lilies are symbols of science and the cosmic expressions of the Life-power. The Magician cultivates lilies because, through observation, we perceive beneath the superficial conflicts of forces presented to us by sensation, there is at work a hidden law of relationship and order. It is the Law of Love. To know the truth is to be free. Beyond doubt, that all the forces of creation are working with every true lover of humanity.

Side by side with the lilies grows roses. They are symbols of love because they are the flowers of Venus. They are also sacred to Bacchus in the Dionysian Mysteries and the god of silence, Harpocrates, the younger Horus. Desire, love, secrecy, beauty, and silence are represented by the symbol of the rose. Furthermore, a cross-section of its flower shows a five-pointed star, the magical pentagram, and the symbol of humanity. Thus the roses in Key 1 stand for human love, in contrast to the lilies, which symbolize the principle of Divine Love that permeates cosmic law.

Therefore 6 stands for universal love and 5 for its human expressions. This is the significance of the cross of six squares (pattern of the cube) to which is affixed a five-petal rose. It is believed by many to be the ancient form of the Rosy Cross.

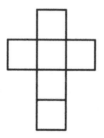

When human desire and affections are related to the cosmic pattern, when humans love as God loves, then our life is the perfect expression of universal laws. Every detail of our day's experience becomes a conscious expression of the Divine Working, the Operation of the Heavenly Sun. This is the real magic.

Magic aims at the expression within the limits of the physical plane. The physical plane is the field of the Life-power's activity, which is within range of the human senses.

These senses are symbolized by the number of roses in the garden - five. They are many-petal, to indicate cultivation and development. They also represent man's desire nature.

Real magic brings the Astral Light to bear upon the cultivation of man's desire nature. Cultivation implies improvement, development, adaptation. Silently and secretly, we purify and prefect our desires. That is, we align our wills with the One Reality. Thus we come nearer to the manifestation of the truth and beauty of the One Reality.

Ageless Wisdom does not offer a way to escape from this world into some other. It puts in your hands the means for the transmutation and transformation of this world. As becomes aware of the significance of your life, you will see the actual world that is hidden from the majority of humanity by clouds of ignorance.

You will find yourself in a different world, and wherever you are, that new world will be. It will be made of the same four elements symbolized on the Magician's table by the wand, the cup, the sword, and the pentacle. It will be a physical world, a world of things and creatures, a world swept by refreshing winds, and lighted by the sun, moon and stars, its lakes and oceans sweet and pure, its substance transmuted by the power of your realization.

The Emerald Tablet tells us plainly that the One Thing's power is integrating if it is turned into earth. The Heavenly Jerusalem in *Revelations* is a symbol of perfected human consciousness, coming down from heaven to earth. All over the world, humanity has been praying, for generations, "Thy kingdom come." In this New Age, many shall see this come to pass.

TAROT INTERPRETATION

Chapter 3

The Builder's Vision

On the Fool's garments are ten wheels, each having eight spokes. The same arrangement appears in the center of the wheel on Key 10, the stars of Key 17, and the sun's rays on Key 19. The arrangement of four lines to form eight angles of 45 degrees is a clue to the right use of Tarot.

We do not select the Keys haphazardly (see below). Every arrangement of nine pictures expresses a specific numerical order. The total number of such combinations is 112. At the end of this course, a table is given, showing them all. Until then, work with a single group of nine Keys in each lesson.

Twenty-two combinations are chosen for your preliminary studies. They are selected with an eye to the underlying intention of this course.

The primary purpose of *Tarot Interpretation* is to enable you to experience the transforming change of consciousness, which will awaken you to a realization of things as they are. The Tarot Keys selected for study and practice are those that are best adapted to bring about this result.

We begin with this combination:

0	1	2
3	4	5
6	7	8

A line can be drawn through the 0, 4, and 8; 1, 4, and 7; 2, 4, and 6; 3, 4, and 5. This forms the double-cross mentioned in the first paragraph. Thus the numbers at the end of each line add to 8 (0 + 8; 2 + 6; 3 + 5). The central Key, 4, in the arithmetical mean (average) between the members of each complementary pair.

In this tableau, the Emperor represents the agency through which the hidden force symbolized by the Fool (Key 0) is manifested as the control of the animal nature typified by Strength (Key 8). The Emperor also stands for the means whereby the self-consciousness (Key 1, the Magician) is brought to the state of mastery pictured by the Chariot (Key 7).

The Emperor is also a symbol of memory (Key 2) is utilized to establish the balance of consciousness and subconsciousness (Key 6).

Finally, the Emperor is the agency whereby the creative imagination (Key 3, the Empress) takes form as the intuitive perception of truth (Key 5, the Hierophant).

Sight is assigned to the Emperor. This applies to mental and physical vision. It is associated with Constituting Intelligence because the power which makes, frames, composes the universe, and regulates all its activities. This is a power of the One Identity, analogous to vision. The Life-power *sees* the universe into existence. Its vision is perfect, and when we see as it sees, we behold a perfect creation.

This is not only a metaphysical perception. Those who see eye to eye with the Creative Mind shares that Mind's power to control the forces of nature on the physical plane. This is the secret of the works of power which characterize the lives of seers and sages.

Perfect mental vision is the perfect reason. The brain of humans is an instrument perfected by the Life-power for the expression of that vision. Thus the sign Aries (♈), governing the head of man, is associated with the Emperor. Through the clear vision formulated in a human's brain, the hidden force symbolized by the Fool is transferred to the heart region, ruled by Leo (♌), and corresponding to Key 8.

$$0 - 4 - 8$$

To the degree that order and right measurement (4) are established, to that degree will the limitless energy of the Life-power (0) be expressed in the perfect rhythm of all the subconscious activities of personal life. When such rhythms are established, the result is mastery (Key 8).

$$1 - 4 - 7$$

Right watchfulness, or concentration, is pictured by Key 1. This is essential to the personal exercise of vision. The follies of the scholastic era demonstrate how barren reason can be unless it is fed by experience. To see, we must look. Those content with superficial observation never achieves a clear mental vision. The characters inscribed on the Book of Nature are plain enough, but we must learn to read them before we can understand their message.

Consider the Emperor as the connecting link between the Magician and the Chariot. Vivid awareness, moment by moment, is a prime characteristic of all masters of life.

Vivid imagery characterizes the speech and writing of masters. They see the law at work in familiar things. They see it here and now. They teach using parables because the meaning of existence is found in the events of every day. The great secrets are hidden in plain sight, and the laws of life are exemplified continually in the affairs of men.

When we see as they see and share their vision, we perceive in the moment is the moment of peace and victory pictured by the Chariot. We recognize that NOW is the acceptable time. Then we understand the words of The Pattern – "Mine is the victorious life."

2 – 4 – 6

Memory enters into the Divine Wisdom. The Life-power's record of past experiences is complete – nothing escapes it. Through the Uniting Intelligence (Key 2), every personal center of the Life-power is linked to the Mind, which never forgets. Our memories are words and sentences of the cosmic memory record. Since they are part of that record, they are written on the scroll of the High Priestess.

As we persist in right watchfulness, moment by moment, our subconscious processes of association link up with cosmic records. Thus we begin to see things in their real relationships, and we estimate every experience at its proper value.

This results in the harmonization and coordination of our subconsciousness with our conscious awareness. By a mental vision, we analyze past events. We come to understand the interaction of self-conscious activities with subconscious life, and the relation of both to superconsciousness, shown by Key 6.

3 – 4 – 5

The Empress is a picture of the positive use of creative imagination. When we reason correctly, subconsciousness is impregnated with our right estimates of the meaning of an experience. Our day-to-day observations of life thus become the seeds of intuition and revelation.

Intuition seems to come from a source outside ourselves, and it does, in a way. However, until we to set our mental house in order, we cannot hear what the Hierophant has to tell us. Today's intuitions are the fruit of yesterday's clear vision.

The Inner Voice is the voice of the Emperor, who assumes the office of Hierophant when the occasion arises. Hierophant and Emperor are

20

not two, but one. The Emperor is the Divine Reason, taking the measure of the outer world of time and space. The Hierophant is that same Divine Reason, conveying to us the eternal significance behind these outward appearances.

Intuition is the subconscious process of *deduction* applied to the elaboration of the meaning of our conscious estimates of experience. Intuition is a consequence of right reasoning, and those who are too careless to watch, too lazy to reason, never hear the Inner Voice.

Look at your combination of Keys again. Notice there are also two other groups – 0, 1, and 2 and 6, 7, and 8. The middle card is the arithmetical mean between the other two.

Thus our little group of nine Keys gives six significant groups of three:

0, 1, 2
0, 4, 8
1, 4, 7
2, 4, 6
3, 4, 5
6, 7, 8

During the next six days, conclude your morning practice by reading the meditation given for that day's combination of three Keys. During the day, keep in mind the statement printed in italics at the end of the meditation. Begin your morning practice, from now on, by looking for five minutes at the week's group of Keys.

Then recite The Pattern on the Trestleboard. After this, write anything that comes to mind in your diary. Finish the practice by reading aloud the meditation for the day. Copy the italicized sentence and repeat it many times during the day.

MEDITATIONS

FIRST DAY: 0, 1, 2. The boundless energy of the Life-power fills my whole being. I concentrate its light-giving power by close attention to this day's experiences. Thus I engrave a clear, sharp record of this day upon the tablets of my memory. *The Life-Breath works freely through me, to invigorate and perfect my whole field of personal expression.*

SECOND DAY: 0, 4, 8. The vision of my heart's desire is a gift of the Spirit, an accurate perception of what is mine now. The perfect order which rules all things is even now adapting suitable conditions for the ideal manifestation of this vision. The mighty forces of my subconscious life are being coordinated for this manifestation. *Limitless Life shows me my goal, sets my affairs in order, and fills me with abundant strength.*

THIRD DAY: 1, 4, 7. All my senses are alert to catch every intimation of the perfect order behind the veil of appearances. The Divine Reason enlightens my mind, for my personality, even now, is a vehicle for the One Power ruling all things. *I am a living witness of the perfect order, which establishes peace and victory throughout creation.*

FOURTH DAY: 2, 4, 6. Everything I remember is a record of the working of the Perfect Law. Every event in my life has its proper place in the perfect order of the Life-power's self-expression. The healing presence of the One Reality harmonizes my activities and my conscious and subconscious minds. The One Reality establishes a balance among them. *Linked subconsciously with every phase of the One Being, I am truly one with the Power, which establishes all things, and shares its knowledge of right relations.*

FIFTH DAY: 3, 4, 5. Today I reap the harvest of yesterday's clear vision and plant the seeds of tomorrow's realization. Today I see eye to eye with God. Today I listen to the Inner Voice and give heed to its instruction. *Filled with the understanding of the Perfect Law, I am guided, moment by moment, along the path of liberation.*

SIXTH DAY: 6, 7, 8. Consciously and subconsciously, I realize the overshadowing presence of the One Identity. My existence is the field of the Life-power's perfect manifestation. The secret force which pervades the universe is my unfailing source of power. *Harmony, peace, and power are mine this day.*

N.B. The two vertical groups, 0, 3, 6, and 2, 5, 8, are intentionally omitted from the exercises because only six meditations are required for a week's work. Try writing a meditation for each of them for your diary.

The Pattern on the Trestleboard

This Is Truth About The Self

0. All the Power that ever was or will be is here now.

1. I am a center of expression for the Primal Will-to-Good, which eternally creates and sustains the Universe.

2. Through me, its unfailing Wisdom takes form in thought and word.

3. Filled with Understanding of its perfect law, I am guided, moment by moment, along the path of liberation.

4. From the exhaustless riches of its Limitless Substance, I draw all things needful, both spiritual and material.

5. I recognize the manifestation of the Undeviating Justice in all the circumstances of my life.

6. In all things, great and small, I see the Beauty of the Divine Expression.

7. Living from that Will, supported by its unfailing Wisdom and Understanding, mine is the Victorious Life.

8. I look forward with confidence to the perfect realization of the Eternal Splendor of the Limitless Light.

9. In thought and word and deed, I rest my life, from day to day, upon the sure Foundation of Eternal Being.

10. The Kingdom of Spirit is embodied in my flesh.

TAROT INTERPRETATION

Chapter 4

The Eternal Teacher

This week's *tableau* is:

1	2	3
4	5	6
7	8	9

The *magic square* for this arrangement is,

4	9	2
3	5	7
8	1	6

OBTW

Paul Case doesn't talk about magic squares until lesson seven, where he lists them. As a student, I found it confusing to flip pages to compare the two squares, so I included them here. A magic square is when the rows, columns and diagonals add to the same value.

In the first few lessons, he uses the *tableau* layout in his text. Later, he switches to the *magic squares.*

Back to the Lesson

In this arrangement, the central agency is Key 5. It is the connecting link between

The Magician (1) and The Hermit (9),
The High Priestess (2) and Strength (8),
The Empress (3), and the Chariot (7),
The Emperor (4) and the Lovers (6).

The tableau shows that the High Priestess (2) is the agency carrying the influence of the Magician (1) into the field of activity represented by the Empress (3). Strength (8) is the agency or means of completing the power of the Chariot (7) in the Hermit (9). The other combinations, 1-4-7 and 3-6-9, will furnish material for your notebook.

In the Tarot Tableau, Keys 1 to 7 are principles, Keys 8 to 14 are laws, and Keys 15 to 21 are conditions or stages of unfoldment. While these designations are correct, as applied to that tableau below, they do not apply to all combinations of the Tarot Keys.

1	2	3	4	5	6	7
8	9	10	11	12	13	14
15	16	17	18	19	20	21

Except Keys 0, 1, 20, and 21, every Key of the series may be interpreted as representing, in some instances, a principle, in others a law, and in others a condition.

Except Keys 20 and 21, every Key may represent a principle.

Except Keys 0 and 21, every Key may serve a law.

Except Keys 0 and 1, every Key may represent a condition.

That is, any Key but 0 and 1 may be the final member of a group of three consecutive Keys like those in the small tableau you are studying this week. Any such Key may represent the outcome, or effect, of the principle represented by the first member of that group of three pictures.

In a group of three, every Key but 0 and 21 may be the middle Key or mean term. This position indicates the law or agency through which the principle represented by the first Key of the series is brought to bear upon the third member of the group.

Every Key but 20 and 21 may be the first member of such a series of three Keys. It represents the principle whose operation is completed through the agency of the second Key and made manifest in the condition symbolized by the third Key.

Thus Key 0 may be representative of a principle in ten instances but will never appear as either agency or effect. Key 1 appears as principle ten times, once as an agency, but never as an effect.

Therefore it becomes evident that Keys 0 to 10 bear numbers, which indicates the number of times each may be taken as representing a law or agency. This rule, however, does not hold good for Keys bearing numbers larger than 10.

Key		Principle	Law Agency	Condition Effect	Total
0		10	0	0	10
1		10	1	0	11
2		9	2	1	12
3		9	3	1	13
4		8	4	2	14
5		8	5	2	15
6		7	6	3	16
7		7	7	3	17
8		6	8	4	18
9		6	9	4	19
10		5	10	5	20
11		5	10	5	20
12		4	9	6	19
13		4	8	6	18
14		3	7	7	17
15		3	6	7	16
16		2	5	8	15
17		2	4	8	14
18		1	3	9	13
19		1	2	9	12
20		0	1	10	11
21		0	0	10	10

From which comes to this rule:

The two members of any pair of Tarot Keys whose numbers add to 21 have each the same total number of aspects.

The Tarot Keys in consecutive pairs, as 0 and 1, 2 and 3, 4 and 5, etc., each member of any pair is the same number of times as principle, and effect. Thus 0 and 1 are both principles ten times, and each is never an effect. 2 and 3 are both principle nine times, and each is an effect once.

By examination of the Keys, The Fool (0) and The Magician (1) are two aspects of one thing. The High Priestess (2) and the Empress (3) are two faces of a single reality. The Emperor (4) and the Hierophant (5) have a similar identity. When the situation depicted by the Lovers (6) is established, it is also represented by the symbolism of the Chariot (7).

Layout the eleven pairs of Tarot Keys. The intimations are striking.

For example, Keys 14 and 15. Generally speaking, Key 14 is a symbol for the idea that every situation or event in your environment results from the operation of the One Identity. Key 15 is a symbol of the appearance presented when the mind of the observer who does not understand the significance of the event. To the eyes of ignorance, the working power sometimes looks like a devil. The understanding of the enlightened sees it as the operative Presence of God.

You will do well to go over the table above several times, slowly and carefully. Layout your Tarot Keys in pairs and write down any ideas that may come to you. The relationships among the symbols are already part of the subconscious content of your mind.

Tarot is part of humanities' inner consciousness as perceived by adepts. It is present in your subconscious, this moment, and always. Your physical Tarot Keys are an externalized from your inner Tarot. Your work with the physical keys brings into self-consciousness the recognition of these interior symbols and their practical meaning.

These details may seem complicated because they are unfamiliar. They are introduced to help you understand how a series of twenty-two pictures are rich in meaning and potent in suggestive influence. Nothing is haphazard in the Tarot's symbolism, nor their relation to numbers and letters.

You are working with tools that were made by masters of wisdom. Let this knowledge give you confidence in the successful outcome of your work. This is indispensable to achieve the best results.

Back to the general interpretation of the groups of three Keys for this week's small tableau:

1	2	3
4	5	6
7	8	9

1 – 5 – 9

When the self-conscious mind is occupied with close observation of the various conditions of the environment, information is gathered (Key 1). These acquisitions of knowledge, valuable as they are, are not sufficient to bring us to the goal (Key 9) without the operation of intuition (Key 5). Observation gathers the facts (Key 1), which the Inner Voice explains (Key 5) so that the seeker for light becomes aware of the truth that all events are the operation of a single Identity (Key 9).

When we have learned to concentrate, self-consciousness collects the reports of our senses (Key 1). Until these reports are coordinated by intuition (Key 5), so their inner significance is evident, we do not perceive the fundamental tendencies of the cosmic operation (Key 9). Therefore intuition (Key 5) is the agency whereby observation (Key 1) is brought to fruition in the adept's realization of the Cosmic Will (Key 9).

2 – 5 – 8

Intuition (Key 5) is also the agency whereby the subconscious record of the fundamental laws of manifestation (the scroll of Key 2) is used to direct the forces of sub-human planes of activity (Key 8). Intuition provides us with knowledge of some cosmic principle or law which applies directly to the solution of an immediate problem.

The knowledge communicated to us by the Inner Voice (Key 5) is the Life-power's perfect memory, which we access at a subconscious level (Key 2). The practical application of this knowledge to the solution of our problems results in the modification of some phase of those deeper activities of our lives, which are symbolized by the lion of Key 8.

Through intuition (5), we recover the Life-power's perfect knowledge of its processes of orderly manifestation (Key 2). This allows for effective modifications of subconscious activity (8).

The stream of our consciousness is continuous with the flow of universal Life-expression (2). Therefore we are instructed by the Inner Voice (5) and gain knowledge of the secret of directing the spiritual powers whose field of operation is in the realm of the subconsciousness (8).

3 – 5 – 7

The development of mental imagery (Key 3) by subconscious processes of deduction and association contributes to intuition (Key 5) and gradually unfolds the realization that personality is a vehicle or instrument for the manifestation of forces above and beyond the level of our consciousness (Key 7).

Below the level of personal consciousness, the deductive process elaborates on our observations and memories, working out their logical consequences (Key 3). The result of this subconscious elaboration of experience (3), is delivered to us using intuition (5). The substance of the intuitional instruction from the Inner Voice is this:

Your existence is a field of manifestation for cosmic activities (7). Your personality is not your Self. There is but one Self. As the Bhargava-Gita says: "Self is the rider in the chariot of the body."

7 – 5 – 3

This knowledge of the true Self and that personality is an instrument or vehicle (Key 7), can be traced to intuitive perceptions in the minds of those who have formulated the knowledge (Key 5.) The sources of these intuitions are deductions elaborated in the consciousness of the person who receives guidance from the Inner Voice (Key 3).

Reason sets our mental house in order (Key 4) so that external relationships are perceived. Intuition (Key 5) carries the process forward, and we become aware of the underlying principles of internal relationships (Key 6). The perception of external order (Key 4) prepares us for the recognition of inner order (Key 6). This recognition is intuitive (Key 5).

An unreasonable individual is one who fails to perceive the real relationships among the events constituting their external environment. Their estimates and measurements are imperfect. Even the Voice of Intuition is misunderstood, on the few occasions when they hear it. In consequence, there is discord in their internal relationships.

They who see the outer world reasonably (Key 4), understand the Voice (Key 5), and their obedience to instruction results in the establishment of the inner harmony pictured by the symbolism of the Lovers.

MEDITATION

For your practice this week, follow the same general plan as last week. Use the Pattern as before, and be sure to have the three Keys for the day placed before you while reading the corresponding meditation.

1st DAY: 1, 5, 9. This day I am alert to gather through every channel of sensation, a clear impression of the events constituting the day's experience. This day I listen to the Inner Voice, which knows and reveals to me the significance of my senses report. From the day's events I learn the trend of the Will of the Eternal, as that Will is manifested, here and now. *I am a witness of the Divine Self-expression. I participate in the Divine Understanding. I am fundamentally one with the Eternal Will.*

2nd DAY: 2, 5, 8. The record of universal law is inscribed on the tablets of my subconsciousness. Whatever I need to know today is communicated to me from that record by the Inner Voice. Therefore I learn today what must be done to make the best use of the mighty forces of my inner life. *The Law of the Eternal, made known to me by the Voice of Intuition, governs every phase of my personal life this day.*

3rd DAY: 3, 5, 7. Today I reap the harvest of my yesterdays. I listen for the inner instruction to show me the true meaning of past experience. I see more clearly that my existence this day is the culmination, and weaving together, of innumerable cosmic activities, continuous with the entire history of the Life-power's self-expression. *The Divine Understanding instructs me and guides me in the way of victory.*

4th DAY: 4, 5, 6. The One Life which rules the universe establishes order in my field of experience. The One Teacher, the source of all-knowing, imparts to me this day what I must know, to grasp the import of this day's experiences. My conscious and subconscious states of personal existence are over-shadowed by the harmonizing presence of the One Reality. *The Eye of the Eternal sees through me its perfect order, the Voice of the Eternal speaks through me its word of truth, the Power of the Eternal establishes in my life its perfect law of love.*

5th DAY: 1, 2, 3. Through my conscious thinking, the Life-power integrates itself in forms of truth and beauty. Keenly alert to this day's experience, I write a clear record of its events upon the tablet of memory. Seeing things clearly, I plant the seeds of understanding. *I watch life intently. I store my memory with vividly realized experience. Therefore, I clarify and make explicit all of my mental imagery.*

6th DAY: 7, 8, 9. My personality is a vehicle of the One Life. The irresistible energy of the Astral Light is coursing through me now. All that I am, all that I do, all that I have, is a direct expression of the One Identity. The One Life lives through me, expressing its mighty power through my being, and leading me along the way, which brings me to perfect realization of the One Identity.

Chapter 5

The Inner Harmony

For this week's *tableau* layout Keys 2 to 10 as follows:

2	3	4
5	6	7
8	9	10

The *magic square* is,

5	10	3
4	6	8
9	2	7

$5 + 10 + 3 = 18$
$4 + 6 + 8 \ = 18$
$9 + 2 + 7 \ = 18$

The sum of the numbers from 2 to 10 is 54.

Rules:

1. When the number on a Tarot Key is the mean arithmetical term between two others, that Key is a link between the other two, and

2. A symbol of the point of equilibrium between the forces the other two Keys symbolize, and

3. A representation of the channel through which those forces act and react upon each other.

For example, 3 is half the sum of 2 and 4.

$$\frac{2 + 4}{2} = 3$$

Thus the Empress is the link between the High Priestess and the Emperor. She represents an activity which equilibrates the forces symbolized by those two Keys. The Empress also typifies the channel which transmits the energy of the High Priestess to the Emperor, and through which the force of the Emperor reacts upon the High Priestess.

These forces are your forces. Keep this always in mind. The calm steadiness of the High Priestess is yours, whenever you let it find expression. Yours are the fertile potencies symbolized by the fertility of the Empress' garden. Your conscious mind, as the composer and regulator of your world, has all the authority and royalty of the Emperor.

The Hierophant is the symbol of Wisdom that guides you aright in every detail of your daily self-expression.

The Lovers portray the eternal relation between your conscious and subconscious minds, overshadowed by the protecting presence of the superconscious.

The Chariot (Key 7) depicts your personality as a vehicle for the One Power, which masters and regulates the mysterious forces of nature.

Strength (Key 8) illustrates the control exerted by your subconsciousness over all the animal, vegetable, and mineral aspects of your make-up and your environment.

The silent watchfulness of the Hermit symbolizes the overshadowing presence of the One Identity, aware of your progress toward union with itself, continually holding up a guiding beacon to light your way.

The Wheel of Fortune (Key 10) is a symbol that every phase of your activity is a manifestation of the perfectly coordinated progress of the cycles of the cosmos.

Tarot speaks by evoking thought. It is also a record of knowledge concerning humanity possessed by great adepts. To look at the Tarot Keys is to impress that knowledge on your subconscious mind, through the natural language of subconsciousness, pictorial symbolism. Tarot speaks to your subconsciousness in its native tongue.

It tells your brain-mind what you are. More important, it shows your subconsciousness the truth about yourself. Subconsciousness then builds the pattern represented by the Keys into a physical structure, gradually altering your psychical and physical composition to correspond to the Tarot specifications. Literally and figuratively, the Tarot Keys are weaving into your flesh and blood. Even though your brain-mind may not grasp the significance of many details of the pattern, your subconsciousness will respond to it.

The study of these lessons will also develop your conscious knowledge of the various elements in your personality. The numeral and other correlations of the Tarot Keys follow laws of thought, practically force the conscious mind to perceive how the various aspects of personality act and react on one another.

Therefore the Tarot affects consciousness and subconsciousness. On the conscious level, it builds up, stage by stage, an orderly and accurate realization of the nature, powers, and possibilities of human personality. On the subconscious level, it brings into manifestation the perfected expression of all your powers, utilizing the body-building functions of subconsciousness. The study of Tarot shows you what you can be, and aids you in the realization of who you are, the Truth about the Self.

Therefore it is essential for you to follow the lessons with the **Keys laid out before you.** *When you read about a Key, look at it.* The words of the chapter will help you understand some part of the truth about yourself. Light rays reflected from the pictures into your eye, after stimulating your sight center, will stir your subconsciousness into activities that will change your flesh and blood in response to the Tarot patterns.

This is the "Operation of the Sun," or a practical work belonging to the "Magic of Light." The light which enables you to see the Keys either comes straight from the day-star itself or is a transformation of the sun's radiance into some other kind of illumination.

2	3	4
5	6	7
8	9	10

The six groups of Keys dealt with in this lesson are as follows:

2, 6, 10
3, 6, 9
4, 6, 8
5, 6, 7
2, 3, 4
8, 9, 10.

You may work out also the meanings of 2, 5, 8, and 7, 4, 1. The general meaning of the six groups selected for interpretation is this:

2 – 6 – 10

Memory is the basis of the grasp of our relation to the cycles of cosmic activity. However, until the relation between the conscious and subconscious minds and their mutual relation to superconsciousness is understood, the memory record will be faulty, and our grasp of the law of cycles will be incomplete.

Memory (Key 2) is more than a record of personal experience. The High Priestess scroll represents a record of the process whereby we come into existence. This part of the subconscious memory record is kept in the cells of the solar plexus (Key 10). Furthermore, subconsciousness must be in the right relation to superconsciousness before the record can be made available for personal instruction (Key 6). The self-conscious mind must know that through the right suggestion, subconsciousness may be opened to an influx of wisdom from superconscious levels.

This is done by attentive listening to the Inner Voice. Within us is a point of contact with the Universal Mind (Key 2), which already knows everything about the law of cycles (Key 10). This Universal Mind (the angel in Key 6) communicates its knowledge to us through the agency of subconsciousness. Whatever part of that knowledge we receive becomes a permanent portion of the personal memory record.

3 – 6 – 9

The limited experience of the senses is not an adequate basis for creative imagination pictured by the Empress. Subconsciousness cannot set our house in order until its reflective power establishes contact with superconsciousness.

This contact can only be established through the conscious mind. It must grasp the law intellectually that subconsciousness is always amenable to suggestion. It must formulate suggestions that set subconsciousness free from sense domination and open it to receive instruction from superconsciousness.

When accomplished, we become aware of the light symbolized by the star in the Hermit's lantern, and we set out consciously toward the goal of union with the One Identity. We understand that union is the result of physiological changes whose roots are in the process of assimilation. We deliberately take up the work of building a new body, a new personality.

Our conscious minds cannot do the building. Its part is to see that the building is begun, that the specifications are laid down, that the materials are assembled for the work. Then the task of actual construction is handed over to subconsciousness, which begins by submitting plans or mental images in the form of desires which embody the essential ideas we wish to manifest.

4 – 6 – 8

These mental images are then subjected to the tests of reason (Key 4). At our present level of development, not every image which rises from subconsciousness is one we wish to realize. Our fertility of invention sometimes exceeds our requirements. The plans must be tested and approved.

This is distinctly the work of self-conscious reasoning, pictured by the Emperor. Keen discrimination is necessary for the respective functions of the two modes of personal consciousness. It is not part of the subconsciousness to criticize. It is her part to produce. Subconsciousness can manifest the weeds of error from old habits and faulty observation or wisdom from accurate observations.

Consider the parable of the wheat and weeds in Matthew 13: 27 – 30.

27. The owner's servants came to him and said, "Sir, didn't you sow good seed in your field? Where then did the weeds come from?"

28. "An enemy did this," he replied. The servants asked him, "Do you want us to go and pull them up?"

29. "No," he answered, "because while you are pulling the weeds, you may uproot the wheat with them."

30. "Let both grow together until the harvest. At that time I will tell the harvesters: First, collect the weeds and tie them in bundles to be burned; then gather the wheat and bring it into my barn."

This is the principle of revision, understood by creative thinkers. Experienced writers, for example, always let their first draft of work come as it will, with little or no attempt at control. It is fatal to give too much attention to matters of detail and form while writing the first draft.

Much practice reduces the amount of waste. When the two aspects of consciousness are balanced in their operation, as shown in Key 6, the original specifications for a given piece of work are usually so definite that the subconscious response to them is accurate. In time, every level of consciousness is brought into harmonious activity, because the reasoned definitions of the conscious mind are correct.

When the suggestions given to our subconsciousness are accurate, then confusion and disharmony are eliminated from the deeper strata of subconsciousness.

5 – 6 – 7

Perhaps the most significant practice is turning over one's problems to the Inner Teacher (The Hierophant). No question is too small, none too great. The act of sitting still and listening for the counsel of the Inner Voice is the most potent suggestion. This practice rapidly develops discrimination. One becomes aware of the presence of the One Self which an ancient scripture describes as "the rider in the chariot of the body." All these good results accrue from the regular, daily practice of the counsel: "Be still, and know that I am God."

2 – 3 – 4

Key 6 is a picture of the relation between Keys 3 and 4. The man in Key 6 looks toward the woman, so does the Emperor look toward the Empress. She is the bringer-forth. He is the inciter of her activity. Memory, like the High Priestess, is a virgin, and therefore sterile. When memory is elaborated by creative imagination (the active composition and development of imagery) in response to accurate, reasonable interpretations of experience, then subconsciousness brings forth a rich store of food for mind and body. Then the imaging process is made richer from by the orderly classifications of reason.

8 – 9 – 10

Similarly, the Hermit, corresponding to the angel of Key 6, has Strength, a symbol of subconscious activities, and the Wheel of Fortune, a conscious grasp of the operation of cosmic cycles, on either side of him in the series of Keys. It is always the light of Universal Wisdom (the Hermit's lantern), which brings about the control of natural forces shown in Key 8. And the state where we are consciously aware of the relation between our activities and the sequences of energy transformation pictured by Key 10 is brought about by the descent of power from the Universal Mind.

MEDITATIONS

1st DAY: 2, 6, 10. My subconscious mind receives the influx of wisdom from superconscious levels. It is continually alert for impressions from that highest source. Its office is to make us aware of my real place in the universal order. *United to the One Life, my thoughts, words, and deeds this day are harmonious expressions of the perfect Universal Order.*

2nd DAY: 3, 6, 9. Abundance in all things is mine. The precious gifts of the Spirit come freely to me through subconscious channels. I am overshadowed by the protecting presence of the One Identity. *Wisdom, right discrimination, and security are mine this day.*

3rd DAY: 4, 6, 8. I establish order in my affairs. I release my subconsciousness from all domination by selfish personal motives. I am strong in mind and body through the establishment of inner harmony. *Order, beauty, and power find expression in my life this day.*

4th DAY: 5, 6, 7. Wisdom itself is my Teacher. By it, I am freed from the delusion of false appearance. My personality is a responsive instrument for the One Reality. *The instruction of the Inner Voice harmonizes all my states of personal consciousness, and victory is mine today over every appearance of adversity.*

5th DAY: 2, 3, 4. Strife is at an end. False appearances have no power over me. I am directed in all my ways by the Supreme Reason. *I am at peace, for Wisdom guides me, and Divine Order finds free expression through my thoughts and words and deeds.*

6th DAY: 8, 9, 10. A tide of power flows through me. I draw ever nearer to perfect realization of the One Identity. My life is one with the Life of all. *Strength, guidance, and mastery are mine this day.*

CLASSICS OF AGELESS WISDOM

Having emptied yourself, remain where you are. – Lao-tze

The wise, knowing through the practice of subjective concentration, the "Effulgent One," extremely difficult to see; concealed deep beyond everything; shining through all acts in every heart; inaccessible, and without beginning; they transcend all pleasure and pain.
– Kathopanishad

Even like the radii fixed in the hub of a chariot-wheel, is He, the Eternal One, permeating everything; and appearing as many, after the forms of the intellect. Meditate on this thy Self as the syllable AUM. May you ever be happy in the realization of THAT, which transcends all darkness. – Mundakopanishad

He thought: I may become many and multiply. He objectified Himself and evolved all this, everything whatever. Having evolved this, He entered into it; and entering became all positives and negatives, all spirit and all matter, all infinite and all finite. –Taittiropanishad

Then, when It was all Unmanifest, It, of Itself, became manifest through name and form, endowing everything with this or that name, and this or that form. This is the import of Its entering into the objective evolved from Itself. – Brhadaranyakopanishad

The God of the twice-born is Fire. The God of the silent one is his heart. Poor intellects find their God in idols. The even-eyed enlightened one sees God everywhere. – Uttaragita

For the Paternal Self-begotten Mind, understanding His works, sowed in all the fiery bonds of love, that all things might continue loving for an infinite time. That the connected series of things might intellectually remain in the Light of the Father, that the elements of the world might continue their course in mutual attraction. – The Chaldean Oracles

But the Paternal Mind accepts not the aspiration of the soul until she has passed out of her unconscious state, and pronounces the WORD, regaining the memory of the pure Paternal symbol. – The Chaldean Oracles

The Paternal Mind hath sown symbols in the soul. Unto some, he give the ability to receive the Knowledge of Light; and others, even when asleep, He makes fruitful from His strength. – The Chaldean Oracles

The Maker of all things, self-operating, framed the world. And there was a certain mass of fire: all these things, self-operating, He produced, that the body of the universe might be conformed, that the world might be manifest, and not appear membranous.

He assimilates the images to Himself, casting them around His form. For they are an imitation of His mind, but that which is fabricated has something of body.

There is a Venerable NAME, with a sleepless revolution, leaping forth into the worlds, through the rapid tones of the Father. – The Chaldean Oracles

TAROT INTERPRETATION

Chapter 6

The Dwelling Place of Spirit

Your study tableau for this week is:

3	4	5
6	7	8
9	10	11

This is the magic square is,

6	11	4
5	7	9
10	3	8

$6 + 11 + 4 = 21$
$5 + 7 + 9 = 21$
$10 + 3 + 8 = 21$

The sum of the numbers from 3 to 11 is 63.

It emphasizes Key 7 as the mean number between the pairs 3 &11, 4 & 10, 5 & 9, and 6 & 8. Besides these combinations, there are 3, 4, 5, and 9, 10, 11, omitting 3, 6, 9, and 5, 8, 11. The first group was interpreted in Lesson 5, and the other will be interpreted in Lesson 9.

The general meaning of Key 7 is Receptivity-Will. This Key represents personality as a vehicle for the directive principle of the universe. Personality is a movable field of action, like a chariot, fenced in by the boundaries of the body and environment. The rider in the car is the real Self. That Self is identical with the power that sets the universe in motion and keeps it going through the various cycles of transformation.

The rider is the One Will. Ageless Wisdom teaches that the will power in human personality is an influx of the directive energy symbolized by the charioteer.

The chariot is the personal organism. It is drawn or moved by two sphinxes, representing the positive and negative phases of sensation. The chariot receives the influx of the universal will-power through subconscious channels, as shown in Key 6, where the woman is the agency reflecting the light of the angel's glory to man.

3 – 7 – 11

Key 7 is a symbol of an agency; the emphasis falls on the car – the personal the body as the vehicle of the One Life. Key 7 is the agency linking Key 3 to Key 11. The influx of the cosmic will-force is the means whereby the image-making power of subconsciousness (Key 3) is enabled to bring about the development of faith. This process adjusts Karma (Key 11). When we are consciously receptive to the influx of the Life-power, and deliberately submit our personal lives to its direction, our mental imagery becomes clear. Our intention to act as vehicles for the One Life is carried to subconscious levels. It works to bring forth from the garden of the Empress the "bread of life" in the form of right desires. Because we imagine accurately, our thoughts take shape in action, adjust our personal lives so that we are harmoniously related to the law of equilibrium.

4 – 7 – 10

Receptivity enables us to receive the direct influence of the universal reason symbolized by the Emperor. When we are correctly receptive, our reasoning is in unison with the Universal Reason.

Then we see things as they are, not merely as they look. Our receptivity puts us in conscious relation with the cycles of universal activity symbolized by the Wheel of Fortune.

To those who do not know this method, it seems that we have unusual command of circumstances, or that we are unusually lucky. We make things occur to suit ourselves. We work amazing wonders.

To ourselves, it seems otherwise. We submit ourselves to the influence of the directive principle of the universe. Then, we find that our daily experience is brought into harmony with the cosmic order. Therefore our thoughts, words and deeds become the specialized manifestation of cosmic tendencies.

5 – 7 – 9

Receptivity enables us to reap the benefits of intuition. Intuition teaches us how to apply a principle which is eternally true, to the solution of a personal problem. The law is universal, but intuition is what enables us to see how the principle is related to the situation which confronts us so that we can change the situation. The more receptive we are, the more intuitive do we become, and the better are we see the path before us. It is the path that leads to a conscious union with the One Identity pictured by the Hermit.

Key 7 is the link between Key 6 and Key 8. By thinking continually of personality as a vehicle for the Universal Will, we experience the harmonious relationship between the conscious and subconscious minds (Key 6). Then we no longer try to bend conditions using "personal will." Instead, we perceive the presence in our lives of the One Will, which is sufficient to meet our every requirement.

The attitude of willingness is a potent suggestion to subconsciousness. It clears away the adverse effects of the wrong ideas that we only have personal powers. The powers assume personal form as they are expressed in thought, speech, and action, but we know that the forces do not have their origin in our personality.

Subconsciousness, acting in response to the suggestion that personality is the abode of Omnipotence, brings the subhuman forces of the personal field into line with the suggestion. Our bodies are altered. The wild beasts of the lower nature are tamed and brought under control. A tide of strength surges through the whole organism, and all the powers of personality are coordinated.

3 – 4 – 5

In sequence 3, 4, 5, Key 4 is the mean or average term. It shows us the power of reason as the link between the subconscious process of mental imagery and the superconscious activities which bring us the instruction of the Inner Teacher.

The deductive method of the subconscious mind forms groups of associated ideas. These are then submitted to the regulative function of self-conscious reasoning, symbolized by the Emperor.

Until our creative imagery of the subconscious has been assorted and classified, we are not ready to listen to the Inner Voice. First, we sort and arrange our mental images; then, we understand the problem. We perceive in what respects we are ignorant.

Until we know what we do not know, we are not ready to seek or profit from the higher guidance from the Hierophant. Intuition gives us light from above, but only when we are prepared to seek that light. Unless we know how to ask, we cannot receive the higher instruction. Until our conscious reasoning has shown us what we do not see, we cannot formulate the specific questions necessary for an answer.

In sequence 9, 10, 11, the Wheel of Fortune as the mean term between the Hermit and Justice. The Hermit is the same as the charioteer, The Emperor, and The Hierophant. He is the guiding power, lighting our path to the heights of spiritual attainment. The mountain whereon he stands is within us, not outside. The path leading to this height is the way of gradual progress in the science of self-knowledge. The Hermit is the goal of our hopes and the foundation of our existence.

The Wheel of Fortune represents the cycles of cosmic law through which the power of the One Identity is communicated to us, its centers of expression. The outcome of the law designated by Key 10 is shown in Key 11. The One Identity adjusts our personal lives through the orderly sequence of its self-manifestation. The more we perceive this, the more are we establish faith. We say, "So be it" to the heavenly order. No matter how things look to us, we affirm that the present situation is an orderly development from all previous conditions.

Faith in the cosmic order is no pretense. It is a logical deduction from our knowledge of the power, wisdom, and beauty of the One Reality. Albert Pike writes:

"Victory is a perfect Success… It is the reconciliation of Light and Darkness, Good and Evil, Free-will and Necessity, God's omnipotence and Man's liberty. It is the harmonious issue and result of all, without which the universe would be a failure." – Morals and Dogma, p. 767.

Our affirmation that the Creative Process is a success includes the realization that we are not yet all-seeing and all-knowing. Therefore, it is logical to assume that apparent failures owe their appearance to our ignorance. Concerning this, Jacob Epstein in *The Sculptor Speaks*, says:

"I do not agree with the theory that the magic wand changes something ugly in nature; transmutation by a painter or sculptor into something beautiful. The thing itself is always beautiful or will appear

54

pleasing to the person who knows how to look at it. The beauty was always there. It is only the accidental circumstances of life that conceal the beauty to some people sometimes and from some people always."

To know how to look at it. That is the thing. We do not agree with Epstein's idea that the inability to look is the outcome of accidental circumstances. Instead, we say that each individual, in due season, enlightenment comes not by accident but by a growth that works outward from within, under the guidance of the One Identity.

* * * *

Follow out the same general plan in your practice this week, as in the previous chapters.

Write out six meditations for yourself.

Chapter 7

The Secret of Power

The Tableau for this week is:

4	5	6
7	8	9
10	11	12

In this arrangement, Key 8 is the central key. The same Keys may be arranged to form a magic square, where the sum of the horizontal, vertical, and diagonal rows are the same. In this magic square, Key 8 remains at the center, but the order of the other Keys is changed,

7	12	5
6	8	10
11	4	9

$7 + 12 + 5 = 24$
$6 + 8 + 10 = 24$
$11 + 4 + 9 = 24$

The sum of the square is 72.

Similar treatment of the tableaus given in Lessons 10 to 13 produces the following magic squares:

0	5	7	4	9	2	5	10	3	6	11	4
4	6	2	3	5	7	4	6	8	5	7	9
8	1	3	8	1	6	9	2	7	10	3	8

Of these, the first, because it includes the zero-sign fails to give a true magic square because the diagonals do not add up to 12. All the others are exact magic squares.

Eliphas Levi says: "The Tarot alone interprets the magic squares of Agrippa and Paracelsus."

"By adding each of the columns of these squares, you will obtain the number of the planet, and, finding the explanation of this number by the hieroglyphs of the Tarot, you proceed to seek the sense of all the figures . . . The result of this operation will be a complete and profound acquaintance with all the allegories and mysteries concealed by the ancients under the symbol of each planet, or rather of each personification of the influences, celestial or terrestrial, upon all the events of life. – Ritual of Transcendental Magic, Chapter 2.

Levi left out of his explanation that only two planets have magic squares, which can be represented by Tarot Keys – Saturn and Jupiter.

Planet	# Rows	# Columns	Magic Square
Saturn	3	3	9
Jupiter	4	4	16
Mars	5	5	25
The Sun	6	6	36
Venus	7	7	49
Mercury	8	8	64
The Moon	9	9	81

There are twenty-two Tarot Keys. Hence no magic square containing more than sixteen numbers can be formed with these Keys.

Fourteen Saturn squares, each containing nine Keys, may be formed. The first of these, including the numbers from 0 to 8, are imperfect in summation, though magic in form. All the others are magical, in both form and summation. The last contains the numbers from 13 to 21, arranged in magic order.

Seven Jupiter squares may be made. The first, containing the numbers from 0 to 15, is an imperfect summation. The others, of which the square containing the numbers from 6 to 21 is the last, are perfect magic squares.

In later chapters, you will find the remaining Saturn squares. Also, the seven Jupiter squares will be explained in the following lessons.

At present, this may seem unrelated to your practical concerns. However, if you layout they keys so that you see their relation to one another, you will find plenty of material for your notebook.

Because the Tarot speaks by evoking thought, it has a special message for every student. Specific arrangements are favorable for this process of evocation. Evocation calls forth ideas from the depths of the unconscious mind. Of all arrangements of Tarot Keys for such work, these magic squares are the most potent.

You will get next to nothing from this information unless you put the Keys before you in the positions indicated. Then, instead of trying consciously to puzzle out what they mean, let your eyes take in what they see.

When you get the knack, you will find your mind tends toward a state resembling reverie. While you look at the Keys, there will be an uprush of perception. Sometimes you don't receive a perception immediately of what the Tarot combination signifies. Other times your mind comes alive, and ideas flash out. Record it in your notebook as soon as you get it. This prevents the loss of many treasures.

Following the regular course of this instruction, the groups of Keys selected for this lesson are 4, 8, 12; 5, 8, 11; 6, 8, 10; 7, 8, 9; 4, 5, 6; and 10, 11, 12. These will be used in connection with the daily meditations.

4 – 8 – 12

The great secret of Key 8 is the subhuman forces of nature are under the domination of human subconsciousness. This control is a present reality, no matter what appearances may be. Even though subhuman forces appear to act adversely, their reaction is an automatic response to states of your subconsciousness. Change the latter, and the reactions are also changed.

A law of subconsciousness is that human life-expression reacts automatically to our subconscious states. This is the secret of our power over conditions. The character of our subconscious states is determined by the quality of our reasoning. First, we reason correctly, so that our estimates of external conditions and our relation to them conform to the universal Constituting Intelligence symbolized by the Emperor. Then the forces which seemed inimical are transformed into allies.

This leads ultimately to a complete reversal of former attitudes. Instead of being burdened with responsibilities, weighed down by a load of our cares and duties, we come to see that we do nothing of ourselves.

This perception does not lead to our giving up action. It involves no loss of interest in life. It does not make us withdraw from active participation in human affairs. On the contrary, it makes our days more interesting. We accomplish far more, with less effort, than we did when we thought we were working alone.

No matter how long you have been trying to do things the wrong way, the whole of nature works in your favor as soon as you let things get done the right way. It stays in your favor, just as long as you retain the right mental attitude.

To maintain the right attitude becomes easier when you trained yourself to listen to the Inner Voice. Take your problems to the Hierophant, and soon you will be aware of its guidance. Take the little problems, as well as the big ones. Build up in your mind, by repeated practice, a confident expectation of being guided aright in all things. Instead of running to human beings for advice, seek the counsel of the Great Teacher.

"In quietness and confidence shall be your strength." (Isaiah 30:15) Obey what the Inner Voice suggests, and the most threatening appearances of antagonism will be transformed into actual aids to your progress and the realization of your desires.

You will gain continually in poise, as your faith in the Intelligence behind all manifestation deepens through your daily contact with it. Don't wait for grand occasions. Don't wait until you are in serious difficulties. Seek guidance always, even when you think you know what to do. When you think you know, it is better to ask the Inner Teacher whether or not your view is correct. This procedure often gives you a second thought far better than your first opinion.

5 – 8 – 11

One of the most typical reasons for apparent failure to demonstrate is that we try to "go it alone." We slip back into the old error that we are living of and by ourselves. Seek confirmation or correction from the Inner Teacher, ask the question, "Am I right about this?" Then act in accord with the decision of the Inner Voice, even when it says "No," is a habit which makes for success.

6 – 8 – 10

When self-conscious, subconscious, and super-consciousness are balanced, the automatic response of the subhuman levels of the Life-power's activity produces the result pictured by the sphinx in Key 10. No longer is one swept away by conditions and the ever-changing flow of circumstance. This is difficult to describe; but though the wheel turns, one does not rotate with it. At the same time, its turning works out for good. Our awareness that human personality is a vehicle for cosmic life has tremendous transforming power at subconscious levels.

$$7 - 8 - 9$$

Key 7 symbolism shows that the true Self is, even now, all that our hearts desire. It has now, and does now, all that we want to have and do.

When this idea takes full possession of us, it becomes evident that nothing can be adverse to us. When the idea becomes apparent to us at the conscious level, our thought and speech are automatically transmitted to subconsciousness, through the memory record.

$$4 - 5 - 6$$

Right reasoning (Key 4) as to the place of personality and its relation to the superconscious life results in the awakening of the inner hearing, which puts us in touch with the Hierophant. We measure our place correctly in the cosmic order. Then our reasoning is transmitted to subconsciousness, and it responds with changes to our bodies. Then we become aware of higher levels of our inner being.

We hear internally and obey what we hear; there are a balance and harmony of the conscious and subconscious, with the superconscious life above the level of personality. Key 6, The Lovers symbolize this.

$$10 - 11 - 12$$

Our awareness of personalities' relation to the cosmic order brings us the realization that our activities are aspects of a universal process. We deepen our knowledge of this truth. Then our faith grows, and we become ever more confident that the Divine Justice is at work in the self-surrender pictured by the Hanged Man.

MEDITATIONS

1st DAY: Keys 4, 8, 12. The Divine Order is established in my life today. All forces of subconsciousness work together for my good. I yield myself entirely to the universal life, of which I am a reflection. *The Power that frames the universe is my strength, and on that Power, I place my sole dependence.*

2nd DAY: Keys 5, 8, 11. Every moment of my life is under guidance from above. Under this guidance, even those forces which appear to be my adversaries are working for me. I am calm and confident this day, in the steadfast assurance that perfect justice is established in all the circumstances of my life. *As I hear, I judge, and my judgment is a recognition of Eternal Justice.*

3rd DAY: 6, 8, 10. Through the reflective power of my subconscious mind, my whole life is filled with light from above. The mighty forces of subconsciousness are at work to fulfill my heart's desire, for I desire nothing but the perfect manifestation of the universal order through my life. *I am free from delusions of false knowledge. I am strong through the perfect coordination of all the forces of my subconsciousness. I am successful because my life is a conscious expression of the universal life, which cannot fail.*

4th DAY: 7, 8, 10. The Master of the universe directs my thoughts and words to deeds of victory. I have dominion over every force in nature, for I am fundamentally one with the Single Identity, which governs all — *the Presence of the Most High dwells within me. The Power of the Almighty works through me. I rejoice that even now, I have my heart's desire.*

5th DAY: 4, 5, 6. I open myself to the influx of the Divine Reason, which sets all things in right relationships. I always listen for the Inner Voice that teaches me the secrets of liberation. My subconsciousness is filled with the light of spiritual understanding. *The heavenly vision is mine; the instruction of Divine Wisdom guides my thoughts and words. This day, the illumination of Pure Spirit shows me the glory of the Perfect Law.*

6th DAY: 10, 11, 12. Not the least act, or word, or thought of mine but has its cosmic significance. Every detail of my experience is an adjustment of my personality for the perfect expression of the power of the One Life. *On that Life I depend completely. The One Spirit works through me to establish perfect justice, and to release me from every form of bondage.*

TAROT INTERPRETATION

Chapter 8

Light from the Height

The Tarot Magic Square for this lesson is:

8	13	6
7	9	11
12	5	10

9 + 13 + 6 = 27
7 + 9 + 11 = 27
12 + 5 + 10 = 27

The sum of all the numbers 5 to 13 is 81.

The summation of these magic squares increases by 3. Thus the tableau given in Chapter 3, arranged in magic form, adds to 12. In Chapter 4, to 15; In Chapter 5, it adds to 18. In Chapter 6, it is 21, etc.

When the summation of a magic square is numerically equal to a Tarot Key, that Key represents the main idea symbolized by the square. When the summation is greater than 21, like 24, 27, or 30, we add together the digits, and the resulting number (theosophic reduction) is a Tarot Key, it is a symbol of the whole square.

In this lesson, the sum 27 is 9 (2 + 7 = 9). Therefore Key 9 symbolizes the main idea of the magic square.

Yod (') is the letter on Key 9, The Hermit. It is a pictograph of a grasping hand. It means:

The actions of humanity, the works of human hands, are expressions of the power of the One Identity. We have no power of our own. No power belongs to us. We are agencies for the distribution of the limitless spiritual energy of the universe.

Our energies are governed by the Law of Response. We do not act of ourselves. We react to impulses rising from the depths of subconsciousness. In Key 9, the higher impulses of the Spirit are represented by the light in the Hermit's lantern.

Most humans leave the power of Spirit out of their thinking. They assume their operating by their energy. Therefore, they self-imposed limits on power. They only include their bodies and visible possessions as their resources. They leave out of the most important part of personal equipment, the real presence of Infinite Spirit, enshrined in the temple of human personality. Because the Infinite Spirit dwells within us, every human being has the limitless resources of that Spirit to draw on.

Our primary resource is the omniscience of the Life-power. The Spirit dwelling within us knows everything. For it, there are no problems, no veils of ignorance and darkness. One of the commonest assertions of the average human being is, "I don't know." Lack of knowledge of what to do, or how to meet an emergency, or the means to carry out some undertaking – such forms of ignorance are personal deficiencies.

We overcome ignorance when we realize that knowledge adequate for our needs is at our disposal. All we have to do is *ask*, and listen for the Inner Voice. The process is simple. We confess our ignorance and listen for guidance, maintaining the mental attitude of confident expectation that our listening will enable us to hear the right answer. OBTW.

If you're nervous and upset, don't be discouraged if nothing comes to you while looking at Key 5. Even if you're troubled, make an effort. If I'm too upset to receive the message, the Life-Power finds another way. For example, two unrelated people tell you the same thing. Or a week later, when you're in the shower, the answer comes to you.

Here the Law of Response is clearly at work. Our listening is a conscious reaction to our knowledge that there is a Voice to instruct us. "Whether you turn to the right or the left, your ears will hear a voice behind you, saying, 'This is the way; walk in it.'" (Isaiah 30:21) The Way shower holds his light on high to illumine our path, and the Voice is ready with wise counsel for those who observe the precepts of its instruction. This way leads to the full fruition of our inherent possibilities, including bondage from death.

The power of the Infinite Spirit enters your life through two channels. These are the conscious and subconscious minds. Your conscious thinking, feeling, planning, and desiring are expressions of the Life-power. The Life-power is also a resource of your subconsciousness. The Life-power is the energy expressed in voluntary and involuntary action. Subconsciousness is the channel through which we make contact with the super-consciousness.

Your conscious mind cannot bear the dazzling light of superconscious mental activity. It receives that light tempered and modified by its passage through subconsciousness. When you release subconsciousness from being dominated by the conscious mind is when you get the best results. This removes the curse of Eve, "Your desire will be for your husband, and he will rule over you."

The curse is not removed by any process designed to let subconsciousness dominate self-consciousness. There is much talk about the evils of inhibitions put upon subconsciousness by the self-conscious mind. However, the power of restraint is necessary because subconsciousness is incompetent to act as the directing agency. Subconsciousness can act as a channel through which the directive power may be brought to bear on us. To take advantage of this, we need only to say to subconsciousness something like this:

"I recognize your function as the agent for the influx of the limitless resources of superconsciousness into my personal life. I renounce all dominance over your activities and turn over your entire operation to the guidance of Infinite Spirit. Henceforth you shall not be subject to me nor to my partial knowledge of the Way of Life. From now on, you shall be an open channel through which the limitless potencies of the Life-power shall flow into the field of my consciousness. You are under the Life-power's all-wise direction. You reject all suggestions of error, which may result from my partial knowledge."

To say this is to put one's whole existence at the disposal of the Universal Life. It is to surrender completely and confidently every detail of one's affairs to the wise guidance of Universal Being.

There are two ways of looking at Infinite Spirit. One is expressed by the noun *immanence* [the divine encompasses or is manifested in the material world]. It is represented by Key 7, which shows Infinite Spirit as the ever-victorious rider in the vehicle of human personality. The other is expressed by the noun *transcendence* and is symbolized by Key 9. It shows Infinite Spirit as a power dwelling far above the level of human personality. These two ideas are not exclusive.

The Life-power is above and beyond what we know or experience at a personal level. Its presence fills the entire universe. There is nowhere that it is not. There is no manifestation of energy which is not dependent on it.

Omnipresence makes the immanence of Spirit inevitable. Since there is nowhere that it is not, the consequence is that it must be here. The Master of our destinies is with us always.

Therefore all the resources of the Infinite are at hand for all us and at all times. Subconsciousness is the channel through which the powers of Spirit enters personality. Therefore subconsciousness is the means whereby circumstances are correctly adjusted. All appearances of injustice and unbalance are due to our imperfect personal knowledge.

Relatively, there are maladjustments, such as poverty, misery, or ill-health. Ageless Wisdom declares that all these painful limitations are educative. Pain prods us into a search for release from suffering. As Henry Wood says, "Pain is friendly." Even when we are not sufficiently skilled in our application of the laws of life to be surrounded by the outward evidence of success, it is profitable to use our statement: "I recognize the manifestation of the undeviating Justice in all the circumstances of my life."

8 – 9 – 10

Ageless Wisdom teaches that all subhuman phases of the Life-power's activity are always under the control of human subconsciousness. We do not have to bring them under control. They are continually under control. The responses of subhuman levels reflect our subconscious mental states. They cannot do otherwise. Even when they seem to be adverse to us and our aspirations, they are responding to the actual states of our consciousness.

If we change our mental states, the responses will change. From the moment we begin to realize that our lives are under the guidance of Infinite Spirit, all subhuman phases of life-expression which constitute our environment will reflect this realization. It will appear to ourselves and others that things have started to work for us instead of against us.

By identifying ourselves with the integrative or up-building phases of the Life-power's action, we go with the current of the Life- power, instead of against it. By the reversal of our mental attitude, we experience a reversal of conditions. In reality, all the sequences of the Life-power's manifestation move on just as they did before, because "with Him, there is no variableness, neither shadow of turning." The change is in ourselves.

5 – 6 – 7

We must establish the habit of listening expectantly to the Inner Voice. That Voice is not loud. It is a "still, small voice," so we must listen before we can hear it. We must bear in mind that harmony between the conscious and subconscious elements of our personality is brought about by releasing subconsciousness from domination by our limited self-conscious knowledge. This release is effected by deliberately surrendering ourselves to the direction of the Universal Spirit. We must practice thinking of that Spirit as an immediate presence in our lives until it is second nature.

When we are responsive to guidance by the One Identity, our daily experience is a demonstration of the One Spirit's power to transform all things into beautiful results.

11 – 12 – 13

Through practice, we accustom ourselves to think of subconsciousness as the agency whereby all conditions are adjusted to bring a maximum of good into expression. As we become habituated to this mental attitude, we find our activity is included in the operation of the Law. Nothing is too small for the Life-power to take care of, nor is anything too great for it to accomplish. Even the transformation of our bodies so that our brains may register the finer types of experience which release us from the bondage of death is included in the operation of the Law. Subtle changes in function and structure happen, so we become aware of octaves of vibration beyond the range of ordinary human experience. We learn through experiments that we are not limited by our bodies to the extent that we seem to be. When we know, the last enemy is overcome.

MEDITATIONS

1st DAY: Keys 5, 9, 13. Infinite Spirit has no problems. It sees what I must do this day. It stimulates my imagination to change the structure of my body, so that it may respond more quickly to the impulses of the One Life. *Instructed by the All-Knowing Mind, overshadowed by Omnipotence, I move on this day toward the goal of perfect realization.*

2nd DAY: 6, 9, 12. My subconsciousness is an open channel, through which the limitless potencies of Universal Spirit are at my disposal. The Hand of the Eternal leads me. I depend utterly on the firm support of the One Reality. *Conscious harmony, the certainty of guidance, and the firm assurance of adequate support are mine now.*

3rd DAY: 7, 9, 11. The Divine Self is not far off; it is a real presence in my life. Its power is beyond all human limits and attainments. Its perfect Law adjusts every detail of my life expression today. *Closer than hands or feet is the One Identity, which now IS all that I hope to become, and this One Life directs all my actions now.*

4th DAY: 8, 9, 10. Human life has automatic dominion over everything below it in the scale of evolution. Human personality is the agent of the Master of the universe. The cycles of cosmic transformation work with me, and for me, because I know this truth. *Mine is the inexhaustible strength of limitless power; mine is the sure knowledge of the Knower of All, mine the perfection of the universal mechanism.*

5th DAY: 5, 6, 7. The Voice which instructs me is not loud, but its message is clear. Its instruction establishes harmony between my conscious and subconscious minds. My thought and words express its perfect wisdom. *Taught by the Divine Mind, harmonized by its healing influence, my life today is a manifestation of its unfailing success.*

6th DAY: 11, 12, 13. The Law works for me, as I work with it. I am firm in my knowledge that the One Life is my perfect support. Even the "last enemy" is, in truth, my friend. *My faith is strengthened today, for I surrender all things to the One Life, and see that Life at work in all the changing conditions about me.*

TAROT INTERPRETATION

Chapter 9

Your Cosmic Life

The Tableau for this week is:

6	7	8
9	10	11
12	13	14

Arranged as a magic square, adding to 30 in every direction it becomes:

9	14	7
8	10	12
13	6	11

The constant summation of this magic square is 30.

$9 + 14 + 7 = 30$
$8 + 10 + 12 = 30$
$13 + 6 + 11 = 30$

The sum of the numbers from 6 to 14 is 90. Notice that the Tableau and the magic square both equal 90.

It indicates that the Tarot Keys are in this group are related to 0 and 3, with 0 as the source of activity, and 3 as the agency of its expression. One of the meanings of this table is the Unmanifested Spirit (0) is the power finding expression through mental imagery (3) in the field of subconsciousness.

Libido is the vitality of undifferentiated Spirit. It is the pure Life-Breath, the sky-power pictured by the Fool. It comes into your field of awareness through subconscious channels. However, it is not the power of subconsciousness. You make contact with it through subconsciousness. Here applies the Hermetic axiom: "That which is above is like that which is below, and that which is below is as that which is above, for the performance of the miracles of the One Thing."

30 reduces to 3, the number of the Empress. Key 3 is a symbol of the main idea in this tableau. It is connected with the meanings of the letter Daleth (ד), corresponding to the Empress. Daleth means "door," and its significance as applied to your work is this:

The activities of subconsciousness in the generation of mental images are the portal through which you pass from your present states of personal experience into those you realize in the future.

You have entered today's set of experiences through this door. Through it, you will pass into the conditions of tomorrow. What you image today will become a pattern for the manifestations of days to come.

This is not obvious to most humans. Many reject it. They say, "I certainly did not imagine the experiences I am having now. How can you ask me to believe that what I imagine now will make any difference in my life tomorrow?"

This would be sound criticism, were all mental imagery produced consciously. Relatively few of your images are deliberately shaped unless you are exceptionally skillful in directing the process. Your subconsciousness generates thousands of images every day. Each image affects your relations with others and your circumstances. Often they do not rise to the conscious level, but they make a difference.

Subconsciousness is the dream-maker. It spins the web of imagery day and night. While awake, we seldom notice the dream process. Our attention is occupied with the impressions of sense experience. Since many of these images affect other persons, both directly and telepathically, they condition the way others react to us and how they oppose or aid us in our undertakings.

You can direct this subconscious activity so that it will work to your advantage. Right now, you manage it from the self-conscious level. The power is already yours. It may be you have been working the controls in reverse.

Your subconscious dream-process is an automatic response to and elaboration of your conscious mental attitudes. By habitually imagining this is a terrible world, that your heart's desire is but dreams, you plant a seed thought into subconsciousness. You plan for failure.

The images may never rise into your field of conscious awareness. They are being developed, and some are amazingly strong.

Your bad dreams sometimes give you terrifying glimpses of the product turned out by your subconscious image factory. Learn how to direct your mental powers, and you will not be bothered by bad dreams. The seed thoughts you plant will not be the kind that grows into nightmare shapes.

Ageless Wisdom says the image-making activities of your subconsciousness are the same, though less potent in degree, as the Universal Mind that brought forth the physical plane. Imagination is the door to external experience. To trace the various elements of your present situation to their subconscious roots is difficult, even impossible. You will do well to remember the principle.

Daleth (7), the door, is also a symbol for the womb. Daleth represents the matrix in which conditions are shaped. This idea is brought out by the details of the Tarot picture of the Empress.

Consider the connection between subconscious imagery and conscious experience. You are not controlled by your subconscious states. You control your subconscious, even when you set into motion a sequence of images whose externalization is unfavorable to you and your projects. The problem is you have been misusing your control. Learn to use it aright, and trouble comes to an end.

76

The principle of control is straightforward. Subconsciousness accepts what we accept at the conscious level. Subconsciousness cannot criticize, cannot reject our conscious ideas. It takes for gospel everything we believe, and it elaborates whatever we give it. From the premises of our conscious mental attitudes, it expands by deductive reasoning.

Because it elaborates your conscious thoughts, you often experience conditions that seem you have not imagined at all. This is where you have to guard against making misinterpretations of experience at the conscious level. You must be on the watch against falling into easy agreement with some other person's ill-considered opinion. Learn to determine for yourself what you accept.

This is particularly important in these days when so many influences play upon us from print, radio, social media, etc. Media companies employ propagandists to plant suggestions in the race-mind. *Deliberate misuse of suggestion to further the purposes of minorities at the expense of majorities is the modern adaptation of black magic.* We see its evil results everywhere.

The multiplication of honest errors by media is almost as dangerous as malicious propaganda. In these days, we need to be prepared to make positive counter-suggestions to the negative statements we hear and read nearly every waking hour of our lives.

Our counter suggestions should be developments of a logical conception of the world we live in. Key 10, the central picture in our tableau and magic square, is important in this connection. It sums up symbolically the main seed thought — it bears fruit in beneficent mental imagery. We begin by thinking through and consciously accepting the idea represented by Key 10. Then, by repeated meditation on the concept, it sets in motion the subconscious creative process, which will eventually lead to our liberation.

Tarot Fundamentals introduced you to these ideas. The emphasis this week will fall on this great seed-idea, which may be put into words as follows:

Your personal experience and action, forces are at work that are more than personal. They are also phases of a cosmic process of a cyclic activity. They move inevitably toward the manifestation of a beautiful result.

Read this italicized paragraph several times. Be sure you grasp its meaning. Right now, you may not give the statement your unqualified agreement. You are not asked to do so. What is essential is to comprehend the meaning of the words. The demonstration of their truth will come later.

6 – 10 – 14

As practice perfects you, keeping distinct the activities of your conscious and subconscious minds, as shown in Key 6. You will begin to notice that your thoughts, words, and deeds are connected with the movement of cycles of energy extending far beyond your present field of being.

Astrology will help observe a regular ebb and flow of mental activity, corresponding to the transits of the moon and planets through your horoscope. When you develop a degree of inner sensitivity, you will become aware of guidance and communication with the overshadowing presence of the angel of Key 14.

7 – 10 – 13

We interpret our activities as an expression of the One Will. Then we understand, in a sense, we are at the spiritual center of the system of cosmic cycles. You will begin to understand that your existence is a continual dissolution of outworn forms, to make room for the unfoldment of new and better ones.

8 – 10 – 12

At first, it may not be easy to maintain the mental attitude we have described, but persist in it. Remind yourself repeatedly of the facts, no matter what appearances may be. In time, you will transfer the idea to subconsciousness, which will begin to act upon it. There will grow in you a feeling that the vital part of you remains unmoved through all the transformations of external circumstances, as unmoved as the sphinx at the top of the Wheel of Fortune. More and more, you will feel the details of your personal life are supported by the cosmic process.

9 – 10 – 11

The word "Self" will change in meaning as you grow in understanding – the One Identity, which finds expression through countless personalities.

You will realize the Self is the spiritual center of the universe and the central reality of your life. It is continually adjusting and balancing the various forces at work within and around you will be reinforced by a host of proofs.

6 – 7 – 8

These changes begin at the conscious level with acts of discrimination. They consist of repeated reminders that the personality is a vehicle for cosmic energy, which is spiritual. Eventually, these repetitions of right ideas as to the correct state of things will establish a new type of response at the subconscious level. Ultimately, these new responses will bring all the subhuman forces of subconsciousness into harmony with the conscious thought.

12 – 13 – 14

It is a willing surrender of one's whole personal existence to the direction of the Life-power. This surrender is expressed in the *willingness to let go of everything, which is no longer an advantage to the progress of the Great Work in one's life.* It is the acceptance of guidance from above, based on the reasoned conviction that such advice is always available.

MEDIATIONS

1st DAY: Keys 6, 10, 14. The two modes of my consciousness work together in perfect harmony. My life is a universal phenomenon, expressed in personal terms. It is directed by the same overshadowing Intelligence that guides the worlds through space. *Poise and supply and guidance are mine this day.*

2nd DAY: Keys 7, 10, 13. I am an embodiment of the Creative Word. Through me, circulate the currents of the Limitless Light. They dissolve in me everything that has outworn its usefulness. *The Word is in my heart, its vibration is the support of all that surrounds me, and it transforms everything into its beautiful image.*

3rd DAY: Keys 8, 10, 12. Even now, my subconsciousness is ordering all forces for my good. I am living at the spiritual center of the universe. I depend on it wholly for power and supply. *The cycles of necessity work always for my good.*

4th DAY: Keys 9, 10, 11. That which I am has already attained all that I hope to be. The whole sweep of the cosmic cycles moves on inevitably to the external manifestation of that attainment. Everything in the universe adjusts itself toward that realization. *The One Identity works through me to balance all the forces of manifestation.*

5th DAY: Keys 6, 7, 8. Consciousness and subconsciousness work in me to manifest the Will of the One Self. My personality is a consecrated vehicle of the Life-power's victorious progress. All forces below the level of my conscious awareness are directed toward the perfect realization of the Great Work. *Ever responsive to the One Life, I share its victorious mastery.*

6th DAY: Keys 12, 13, 14. I depend utterly on the Perfect Law. I let go of all that binds me to the past. I set my feet firmly on the path, which leads to the heights of Self-realization. I am utterly free, for I do nothing of myself.

TAROT INTERPRETATION

Chapter 10

The Secret of Balance

The Tableau for this week is:

7	8	9
10	11	12
13	14	15

Arranged as a magic square, adding to 33 in every direction, it becomes:

10	15	8
9	11	13
14	7	12

$10 + 15 + 8 = 33$
$9 + 11 + 13 = 33$
$14 + 7 + 12 = 33$

The sum of the numbers from 7 to 15 is 99.

Layout the Keys for both combinations. Then look at them, with pencil and paper at hand, so that you may make a note of anything that may be suggested to you. You never can tell when you will tune in on the thought of somebody who knows a great deal more about Tarot than you do.

If you persevere, you should find yourself getting this mental radio from members of the Inner School. More and more often, the best knowledge of the Tarot will come to you this way. The secrets are never printed in books or lessons. They are communicated directly to persons having sufficient receptivity.

The simplicity of the methods whereby one becomes receptive deceives many and keeps them from persistent practice. Pencil and paper, or some other means of keeping a record, are necessary. The impression made by these brainwaves is often fleeting as a dream and passes beyond recall unless one captures the message at the moment it comes.

If you prepare these impressions, the practice will give you verification of the existence of the Inner School. You accumulate evidence that the source of these flashes of enlightenment does not come from your personality, conscious or subconscious.

It is not easy to describe. There is a difference between one's thought and what is received telepathically, distinct as the difference between the sound of one's voice and that of another person. After you receive these mental radiograms, it will be evident that they come from different types of mentality, which may easily be distinguished, one from another.

We know that every reader of these pages will not enjoy this contact with the Inner School. Experience shows that no matter how we insist on the importance of following strictly the simple directions for using Tarot, it is the exceptional student who does what they are told.

These instructions are not one man's opinions. Instead, they are concentrated research and experimentation carried on for centuries. Many students feel that they know the Tarot and what to do better than we do. We do not coerce others' beliefs or actions. However, these pages do not contain our personal views about methods and practice. We are transmitting to you something we have received and tested carefully. Therefore, we know it will work if you will work it.

7 – 15 – 11

In the first group of three Keys in this week's tableau notice first the Warrior (7) and then the Adversary (15) with Justice (11) between them. The Warrior is not fighting, and the sphinxes of his car are at rest. In Key 15, the chains around the necks of the two figures would not hold them a moment, if only they knew enough to lift the loops over their heads. Nowhere in the universe is there anything like the Devil. There are no problems for your true Self, the Warrior in the chariot, nor is there an Adversary. The symbol of Justice, with the scales, is perfectly balanced, shows the reason. Since the forces of the universe are always in perfect equilibrium, there is no antagonism anywhere, except in appearance. The wise see this. Others try to reform the world.

8 – 11 – 14

In the next group of three (8, 11, 14), the meaning of Key 8 may be taken as a reference to the Emerald Tablet: "This is the strong force of all forces, overcoming every subtle, and penetrating every solid thing." That force is now at work bringing about the realization of your heart's desire. Never mind any appearance to the contrary.

To study these lessons indicates you have reached the point in your spiritual development where you are about to be released from the hypnotic spell cast by appearances. The force at work through you is adequate to overcome the subtlest of your seeming adversaries and to penetrate enough to reach you through every apparent obstacle.

You are nearing the time when you will see that this force is being employed to make fine adjustments that are required to bring you to your goal in life. Before long, you should begin to understand that your life story is a mental conception of the Author of All.

You will understand that what you thought you wanted for yourself is something the Life-power wants for you and is working through you to bring into actual manifestation.

Ageless Wisdom teaches the universe is an expression of Conscious Energy. It follows that the One Intelligence sees the whole of its manifestation, and every detail thereof. Time does not bind it as we are bound, as long as we are limited by the sense of succession, which is characteristic of our self-consciousness. As Abbe Dimnet says, in *What We Live By*:

"Pure Spirit, God, all the time, sees the whole picture of which we see only fragments. The Universe, even the endless succession of universes which astronomy has sometimes inferred from the conservation of energy, is present to Him as our consciousness of ourselves is present to us."

9 – 11 - 13

Cosmic Intelligence includes the thoughts and desires of every human being. The One Identity is all the power there is, and the whole of that power is related to the manifestations of your personality. Therefore your personal life is an aspect of the continuous process of the Life-power's self-adjustment. Adjustment means there is a continual dissolution of forms. They are a continuous series of structural disintegrations, but this eternal transition from one form to another expresses a power which itself suffers no change in essence. No structure or condition can arrest your progress, because the real YOU is essentially identical with the One Reality.

10 – 11 – 12

Manifestation is pictured as a system of wheels. "Wheels within wheels," Ezekiel says, intimating an intricate correlation of cycles, like the symbolism of Key 10. Understand that this system is not a mere mechanism, Ezekiel says, "The wheels were full of eyes." The Great Rota is an intelligent expression of life.

Amid all the whirling, there is a balance. Every degree that the wheel turns upward on one side is compensated by an equal degree of descent on the other. At the center, there is absolute stillness. They who find the CENTER, the abode of Pure Spirit, are freed from the necessity for action. It is ended for those who become like a pendulum, which has ceased its motion. Thus it is forever true that the wise man thinks, "I am doing nothing."

7 – 8 – 9

Tarot is intended to effect a change in the student's interpretation of the meaning of an experience. As astronomy has corrected our ideas of the movements of the heavenly bodies, so does Ageless Wisdom correct our opinion of the nature of our activities. The uninitiated think personal action is self-originated. The wise consider personal action is the localized expression of universal forces. They flow into and through the field of personality, like the river pictured in Key 7.

Most persons look upon the forces surrounding them as being alien and dangerous, like the lion in Key 8. However, we continually exert control over these forces. They respond automatically to our conscious attitudes, even when we apply that control to bring us painful (and therefore, educative) experiences.

Most humans look at the goal of attainment as in the future and bound up with environmental conditions. The instructed see that the goal is the realization of the One Identity is closer at hand than anything else. This is all that anyone ever hopes to be, have, and does all that anyone ever wishes to do.

Included in a reversal of interpretation is freedom from the fear of death. Once a student has experienced this reversal, they understand that their personality will survive the death of the physical body. The personality is independent of your body, even while our bodies exist.

This is real knowledge, gained by experiment, and subjected to tests as searching as those applied to any other type of scientific investigation. In the course of the experiments, many difficult problems are met and solved. Consequently, the conviction grows in the student that whenever the forces of the universe present him a forbidding and adverse appearance, it is because they have not yet learned the true meaning of that appearance. There is no power inherently hostile to their welfare.

Summary

Tarot was invented by wise men and women to make others wise as themselves. These Keys are a symbolic summary of the understanding of Those Who Know. By looking daily at these pictures, you impress your subconsciousness with a condensed statement of the attitude toward life and its problems, which enables adepts to perform their mighty works.

An adept doesn't acquire special powers. They achieve a unique point-of-view. The masses accept the universe at its face value, but the adept discern what the actual state of things.

Use Tarot as these lessons instruct, and you will saturate your subconsciousness with the wisdom of the Inner Circle of Those Who Know.

Your subconsciousness will respond automatically to this treatment. First, it will make you see things differently and produce a change in your interpretations and your emotional attitudes. Ultimately, it will build you a new kind of organism, through which the forces of the universe may be expressed in works of power.

MEDITATIONS

1st DAY: 7, 11, 15. My real Self has no problems. My faith is steadfast in this conviction. The mask of the Adversary hides the face of the Beloved. *I have nothing to fight, for perfect adjustment even now overcomes every seeming evil.*

2nd DAY: 8, 11, 14. The strong force of all forces is at work in me. It cuts every knot of difficulty. It is the free power of my true Self. I am filled with power, adequate to my every need, and I face this day as an opportunity to prove the truth on which my faith is founded.

3rd DAY: 9, 11, 13. Pure Spirit, my true Self, sees everything as it is. It remains poised amid action. It dissolves every limitation which might retard my eternal progress. *My life is in the hand of the Eternal, and its perfect Justice loses all my bonds.*

4th DAY: 10, 11, 12. The Center of the cosmic whirlings is the Center is also the center of my existence. That Center is in perfect equilibrium. I am at rest as I rest in it. The wheel of manifestation has stillness at its center, and that stillness is in my heart of hearts.

5th DAY: 7, 8, 9. Ageless Wisdom corrects all my false notions about the meaning of my life. I live by the power of the whole universe. My goal is knowledge of the One Identity. *My true Self masters all the forces of nature now, and stands alone and unmoved amid all appearances of struggle and effort.*

6th DAY: 13, 14, 15. Death is the name given by ignorance to change in form. I am in the midst of an experiment which releases me from that ignorance. The problems I face are but veils for the one beautiful Truth. *I pass on from stage to stage of the Great Work, which dissolves every appearance of evil and restriction.*

TAROT INTERPRETATION

Chapter 11

True Surrender

The Tableau for this week is:

8	9	10
11	12	13
14	15	16

The Magic Square is:

11	16	9
10	12	14
15	8	13

$11 + 16 + 9 = 36$
$10 + 12 + 14 = 36$
$15 + 8 + 13 = 36$

The sum of the numbers from 8 to 16 is 108.

At the center of both arrangements is Key 12, the Hanged Man. The constant summation of the magic square is 36. It shows responsiveness (Key 9), expressing the power of discrimination (Key 6), through creative imagination (Key 3). Key 12 represents the means for balancing the forces symbolized by these Keys. Key 9 shows the outcome.

Notice the many complementary opposites shown in the tableau. Key 12 represents the central agency that carries the actions and reactions of 8 & 16, 9 & 15, 10 & 14, 11, & 13. Key 11 balances Keys 8 and 14. Key 13 balances Keys 10 and 16. Study the groups of three Keys and record what they suggest.

The different arrangements of Tarot Keys show how the forces they represent act and react on one another. No single force is isolated. TAROT as letters is the Latin ROTA, a wheel. Every part of a wheel is related to every other part. The parts move together. The force symbolized by the Tarot Keys are interrelated. Therefore the make-up of the Tarot shows that all the activities of our lives are aspects of a fundamental unity.

The higher spiritual consciousness enables us to comprehend the Whole. Our intellectual mind discerns only the parts. The divisions and separations are in the mind, not in Reality. This is the most important lesson of Ageless that serves to correct a brood of errors.

$$8 - 12 - 16$$

The consciousness attributed to Key 8 is The Intelligence of the Secret of all Spiritual Activities. First of all, it means that there are no unspiritual activities. Everything in your experience expresses the power of the Life-Breath. **The secret pictured Key 8 is the subhuman expressions of the Life-Breath are subject to control by human subconsciousness**. This truth is of great importance to a practical occultist. It will enable you to utilize an unlimited supply of energy. It is the secret of power.

As a rule, the conscious mind learns from a teacher. Very gifted observers learn it by watching nature. Once perceived, this truth becomes a new foundation for our interpretations of experience. True also is subconsciousness is amenable to control by suggestions originating in the conscious mind. That is the absolute subordinate to the subhuman levels of the Life-powers activity. Therefore our work begins in the conscious mind and our ways of interpreting experience.

Key 12 is the consciousness that creates results opposite to those we find restrictive and painful by reversing our conscious attitude toward life.

Hanged Man tells us. "I have not done these things. They were accomplished by a power higher than myself, working through me."

The thoughts and actions of these individuals are misunderstood. They terrify lesser minds. Often they are considered to be enemies of society. Their ideas and practices are condemned as a threat to existing institutions.

In a sense, this is true. If all humanity lived as these few live, the present state of society would be overthrown. The existing social order (or disorder) is founded on fear and the delusion of separateness. *It is a system of organized selfishness.* Among human beings released from the bondage of fear, this reign of greed and terror ends. It is based on the lie that any man may live for himself alone.

Ageless Wisdom says everything is under the supervision of a benevolent Universal Consciousness. It means the world and its events express the Will of a single Knower. It counsels us to place our complete dependence on this Will. Those versed in the practice amaze their contemporaries with a command of the forces of nature. As Jesus put it, they do the will of the Father. A child can grasp this idea and put it into operation. It is too simple for persons caught in the web of delusion. Such persons point to the semblance of evil and ask how, if there be a benevolent Supervisor over such conditions, the critics call "grim realities." They ignore those who apply themselves to living a life of surrender are happy and healthy, find their every need supplied, and genuinely enjoy themselves.

The critics pooh-pooh the esoteric doctrine that "grim realities" are instead waking nightmares, produced by a sort of hypnosis that affects certain levels of the race-mind. They are victims of hypnotism. They are like persons having a bad dream and cannot perceive that it is preposterous.

Sooner or later, they will awaken to the truth. Their arguments need not disturb us. After all, Ageless Wisdom can cite a long line of successful men and women who say that their secret was surrender to the guidance of the One Will.

Comprehension of cycles is the root-idea of Key. When you understand the significance of your personality, and its relation to the universal order, you can employ this knowledge as a means to effect your release from bondage. Then all the forces of the cosmos are ready to work for you. Our states of body and circumstance depend on our comprehension of relationships. The connection is not obvious, and the natural man prefers the obvious.

There is a way beyond the limitations of the natural man – surrender. Hence we find the theme of renunciation running through the books of wisdom. What is renounced is a delusion – the error that any human being is separate from the benevolent order of the universe. When the practice is made a subconscious habit, then one becomes increasingly aware of the guidance of a Higher Intelligence. Then the way to ascent, which leads to the perfect blending of personal aspiration with the Cosmic Will.

For surrender, faith is required, but not blind faith, based on unquestioning acceptance of dogma. It is reasoned faith, growing out of imaginative development of knowledge available for those who master the technique of analyzing what goes on in their environment and their inner life.

Lack of attention is responsible for our erroneous opinions. Hence we draw false conclusions from faulty observations; then, wrong conclusions become premises. Our subconsciousness elaborates by deductive reasoning into systems of error and defeat. If we practice concentration, so that we observe accurately, we read the message of the book of nature.

When we observe correctly, we store our memories with correct representations of reality. Then we make correct deductions, and the fruit is a faith that nothing can shake. Out of that faith comes full surrender to the inevitable perfection of the cosmic process. As a consequence of our submission, even death loses its terrors, transforms its dreadful countenance, and at last, is overcome completely.

You cannot overly remind yourself that subconscious response to mental attitudes held by self-consciousness is entirely automatic. Subconsciousness is like a garden. If you plant weeds, it grows them just as vigorously as if you plant flowers. It has no choice. It can offer no opposition.

Do not concern yourself with practices designed to overcome subconscious resistance. The correct procedure consists in repeating the assumption of right mental attitudes again and again until new habits have been formed. It is like learning to maintain a proper bodily posture. At first, there are many relapses into the old wrong attitudes, but, as time passes, and effort continues, these become less and less.

The most fruitful thought on which you can dwell is symbolized by the Hermit. This thought should be part of your daily life: *The Hermit is the overshadowing presence of One who knows, understands, and lights the way for your upward progress.* Made habitual, this thought works subconsciously to bring you into harmonious adjustment with the sweep of the cycles of cosmic activity. Then you'll find the wheels within wheels of the Life-power's manifestation working together to ripen to fruition the realization of your aspirations.

Continue to endeavor to purify your theories should be your aim. People are always saying: "All this sounds so true, when I hear it at a lecture, or read it in a lesson. But how can I, when I return to the world, make it work?"

First of all, try to keep some part of your consciousness from ever returning to the world. The truth of things is not to be found on their surfaces. Try acting as if these doctrines of Ageless Wisdom were true. Remember, thought is action. Let yourself be directed by what Key 14 pictures as an angel. Pause many times a day to remind yourself of this guidance. Nothing is too small or great to turn over to it.

Try it, and you will soon find this out for yourself. In every day's activities, all sorts of problems arise. Remind yourself continually that, however terrifying they may be, these appearances are due to your ignorance of some factor involved.

The ignorance is personal. Your real Self already knows the right answer. The more you invite its direction, the speedier you will come to the solution to your difficulties. You will probably have to abandon some opinions long-held.

It may be necessary for you to demolish structures of error. In due course, there will be less and less conflict. Keep on exercising yourself in right thinking. Eventually, you will reap from your subconscious mentation an abundant harvest of constructive realizations.

MEDITATIONS

1st DAY: Keys 8, 12, 16. Every activity in my world is a spiritual activity. Every particular manifestation of this activity is related to every other, and each depends on the whole. Nowhere is there any real separateness or isolation. *The One Spirit is my sole support: its power demolishes all structures of delusion.*

2nd DAY: Keys 9, 12, 15. My life and its needs are fully known to the One Identity. I rest calmly in this knowledge. I meditate on it daily and hourly. *My way is lighted by the lamp of Wisdom: as I still the tumult of my thinking, that light shines like a star, to lead me onward.*

3rd DAY: Keys 10, 12, 14. Every cycle of the Life-power's manifestation brings me nearer to my heart's desire. Let me be free from all sense of struggle. The law of perfection is now at work in all my members. *The wheel of manifestation turns round the still center where I stand at rest, filled in mind and body with the power of the Eternal Presence.*

4th DAY: Keys 11, 12, 13. All waste is eliminated from my life experience. I do nothing of myself. The Life-power is transforming me, moment by moment, into a perfect image of itself. *Poise is mine this day, and peace, and I see that every change is for the better.*

5th DAY: Keys 8, 9, 10. All the forces of subconsciousness are at my prompt command. I am a direct channel for the Master and Supervisor of the universe. My place is truly at the very center of the wheel of existence. *Nothing is or can be my antagonist, for I am one with the Divine Essence at the heart of all things.*

6th DAY: Keys 14, 15, 16. The path of supremacy is open before me. Whatever be their masks of terror, I fear no appearances, for I see that there is no separateness anywhere. *Joyfully I accept every test, meet every problem confidently, for I know I cannot be separated from the Wisdom and Goodness of the Eternal.*

TAROT INTERPRETATION

Chapter 12

Perpetual Transformation

The Tableau for this week is:

9	10	11
12	13	14
15	16	17

The magic square is:

12	17	10
11	13	15
16	9	14

In both arrangements, the central Key is 13, Death, The constant summation of the magic square is 39. It shows reversal (Key 12), expresses the Law of Response (Key 9) by the agency of creative imagination (Key 3). Key 13 represents the means whereby the forces symbolized by the pairs of opposites in the tableau are balanced. Key 12 shows the outcome of the equilibrium.

The meanings of this tableau revolve around the idea of change symbolized by Key 13. There is a sense that Key 13 relates to the phenomenon of the cessation of a particular personal existence on the physical plane (Death). The Bible says that the last enemy to be overcome is death. It also refers to other esoteric doctrines.

Ageless Wisdom teaches the processes that bring the death of a body are expressions of laws and forces when understood, release us from the bondage to death. When we know what makes us die, we learn the secret of eternal life.

Because of humanity fears death, little progress has been made in this branch of occult knowledge. The few who have looked death in the face have reaped as their reward the revelation of a priceless secret. This is what the alchemists mean by saying: "Dissolution is the secret of the Great Work."

This week examine Key 13. Then review the explanation of symbols. Give thought to the rising sun. Open your inner ear to any suggestion which may come to you from the Inner School, concerning the seed symbol in the upper left-hand corner of the picture.

When the Keys are laid out in the tableau, this seed in Key 13 seems to point upward toward the Hermit; but in the magic square, it points toward the Hanged Man.

In this connection, consider all you know about the letter Yod (ʼ) and the Hermit, and the significance of the element of water. Observe that the rising sun is one of the stars pictured in Key 17.

Consider Keys 10, 12, 16, and 14, as they are placed in the tableau. At the top, a symbol of the turning wheel of time, with the unmoved sphinx, a symbol of the spirit of humanity, sitting still while the wheel turns (Key 10). At the left is the Key 12 showing human personality as the temporary suspension of the whirling forces of the universe, by the condensation of those forces into a particular form.

One of the meanings of Key 12 is personality is like a whirlpool. It maintains its identity because of forces flowing through it, and when these are turned in another direction, the whirlpool of personality disappears. Our apparent stability as entities on the physical plane is temporary.

We fall into the error, supposing the physical plane existence to be our whole being. If we let this error develop into the delusion that human life on the physical plane is an isolated fact, unrelated to cosmic manifestation, then, death is the terror and destruction pictured by Key 16.

Wise counsel and specific experiments aid us in overcoming delusion. Then we see that physical existence is an incident in our total life expression. The open way shown in Key 14 will take us to the heights of spiritual realization.

9 – 13 – 17

It is the energy of the Primal Will, symbolized by the light in the Hermit's lantern, at work in the processes the break down the human body. The breakdown of tissue releases this energy in forms of our activity, thinking, feeling, doing. A sage who sits motionless in meditation is engaged in action, and one evidence is the work in mental control by concentration and meditation makes the body perspire freely.

Intense mental work leading to the perception of higher forms of reality is work that breaks down cells similar to muscular effort. Perspiration eliminates fatigue poison, which is a consequence of the disintegration of cells.

Look at the tableau. In Key 10, notice the two wavy lines (♒) at the bottom of the wheel, over the R. The Aquarius symbol (♒) is over Key 13. It is also the alchemical symbol for dissolution. In Key 10, the head of the man is a symbol of Aquarius. The man's head is in the same position as the seed symbol in Key 13. This is also the place occupied in Key 16 by the falling crown.

Humanity is the seed form of a state of life manifestation *beyond ourselves*. The lightning struck crown of creation in Key 16 is a symbol of an error. In a sense, the essence of human life is identical to the one great Reality. The error is in the belief that the Great Work is brought to completion by the appearance of the "natural man."

When the human race loses its vision of the Beyond, then confusion and terror come. Read the Bible story of the Tower of Babel. The desire to build a memorial to present glory caused the trouble. On Key 16, you will see the error depicted. The Tower is a symbol of a vain attempt to arrest the onward flow of the Life-power. It represents the sum-total of the errors growing out of the folly of supposing that humanity, at its present level of development, is the be-all and end-all of the creative process.

Human personality is a stage of that process. Beyond this stage lie untold and unguessed glories. Few every generation grasp this truth. They have verified it and passed beyond the limitations which the majority supposed to be fixed, unalterable laws. Some persons know the past and the future, as well as the present.

Some persons can read the innermost secrets of the human heart. Others are not restricted to the one spot on earth where their physical body happens to be. Some have caught a glimpse of the possibilities of this seed form we call Humanity. I have received small but definite assurances that our limits are not so fixed as once we believed.

Exoteric dogmas have their germ of truth because they are veils for deeper meanings. We may smile at the idea that death is the gate to heaven, where all the injustices rampant on this globe will be made right. In a sense, it is true that by dying we enter the heavenly world where evil ceases to hold us in bondage. Have you stopped to think that the person who began the study of these lessons is no more? To the degree your study has brought enlightenment, is degree the disintegrative process symbolized by Key 13 had eliminated a portion of the person you were when you began your studies.

Problems that terrified you then have been solved. Difficulties are overcome. You can see the working of justice in situations that formerly appeared to you to be unmixed evils. Your reasonable faith enables you to look forward to further adjustments.

You understand the bondage you seem to be enduring is a result of ignorance. And ignorance is a resistance of certain parts of your physical organism to the passage of the light of the Life-power's perfect knowledge of all things. By dying to the old personality, you are glimpsing your place in the great cosmic order. That place is the real "heaven" where no unrighteousness can enter, where sorrow is at an end, where perfect justice is the unvarying rule.

Using a whirlpool as a symbol for existence on the physical plane, a vortex is in a state of intense activity. The working power behind the activity is the flow of the river through the whirlpool. So it is with human life. False mysticism is the refuge of deluded souls who fancy that by refusing to engage in action, they come closer to Reality. Such persons try to avoid doing what their hands find to do. Realization is what is pictured by the Hanged Man; the motive power does not reside in the personality.

One suspends the false notion that what one does is self-originated. True mystics are never Quietists. Many of them are prodigious workers. None are shirkers. Some work with their brains and nerve centers, rather than with their hands, but just the same, they work. In all they do, they are aware that their activity is but a phase of the world process.

This mental attitude is favorable to the subtle changes in body chemistry connected with Scorpio and corresponding nerve currents. Your mental attitude brings about the awakening and activation of higher brain functions. The consciousness of the person changes. He dies to the old man, and rises again into ah higher order of knowing called "The Knowledge and Conversation of the Holy Guardian Angel."

"Angel" means messenger. The angel having charge of the unfoldment of your life may not be anything like what you imagine angels to be. There are angels and angels. There is a center of the Life-power's expression, which is the means of leading you higher is your particular angel for this stage of your journey along the Way to Freedom.

9 – 10 – 11

The fundamental doctrine of Ageless Wisdom is *All forms of life expression are vehicles of the One Identity*. Behind and above your particular "guardian angel" for the present moment, is the over-shadowing perfection of the One Identity. He/she that is entrusted with the work of supervising the current stage of your progress is a messenger and representative of the Supreme One.

The journey you are making toward the heights is the Way of Return. It is the upward arc of the wheel of manifestation. You and the rest of humanity are like Hermanubis on the Wheel of Fortune. Your spiritual eyes are beginning to catch glimpses of the glorious Beyond which the Fool sees (hence the eyes of Hermanubis are level with the letter A, or Aleph א.) Your spiritual ears are bringing you an inkling of the truth that your real being is one with the ONLY ONE.

Your faith is confirmed by experience and founded on reason. You do not believe blindly. Ageless Wisdom says: "Come, let us reason together." It shows you the relationships among the phases of existence which are passed over by most persons. It sharpens your powers of observation. It points out the footprints of the Master Principle and develops your creative imagination so that you can see with the eye of faith what your physical eyes have not yet witnessed.

On its practical side, it is enabling you to make adjustments in your thinking and teaches you how to direct your emotional life into better channels of expression. All this is gradually making you into a new person. What you were is passing away. What you are is better than what you were.

As your spiritual vision grows keener through creative imagery, you will understand the saying: ''Beloved, now we are children of God, and it is not yet revealed what we would be. But we know that, when he is revealed, we will be like him, for we will see him just as he is." – John 3:2.

The world of natural men and women see Him as He is not. Therefore, the "God" of exoteric theology is more devilish than divine. Thus the fearful image of the Devil in the Tarot is a picture of God misunderstood or seen mentally as He is not. This vision of terror has been conjured up by the collective imagination of the natural man, who looks with dread on anything which seems to threaten the continuance of fixed states of existence. The natural man puts their trust in form and seeks the perpetuation of form. Therefore they fear change, dreads novelty, detests difference. Conformity is their fetish. When anyone dares to be different, the natural man will go to any length to suppress the innovation and get rid of the innovator. This is all too prevalent, even in our supposedly enlightened times.

Examine the picture of the Devil. He represents all that does not "fit in" with our comfortable preconceptions. But the Life-power is not limited by our ignorance. It is always presenting us with new appearances, which seem to be exceptions to our notions of order.

Therefore the natural man personifies unknown activities as the demon and ascribes their failures to the malicious influence of the Adversary.

MEDITATIONS

1st DAY: Keys 9, 13, 17. The powerful and irresistible energy of the Primal Will courses through me. It breaks down every obstacle to its onward movement. It opens my understanding so that I perceive the beauty of the Great Pattern of manifestation. *The One Identity transforms me into its likeness and opens my eyes to the wonders of its Perfect Law.*

2nd DAY: Keys 10, 14, 16. I am ascending into a higher order of being. This day is a day of change from the imperfections of the past into a closer approach to the Divine Reality. The lightning-flash of inspiration overthrows my mistaken structures of ignorance and prejudice. *I am an expression of eternal progress and transforming the power of life, which breaks down every prison house of ignorance.*

3rd DAY: Keys 11, 13, 15. Mine is a reasoned faith. I die daily from the misapprehensions of the past. I begin to see that evil a seeming injustice are but aspects of the Good, stages of the Life-power's unfoldment which I have yet to understand. *I am a center of the power of cosmic adjustment which overcomes and transforms into beauty every appearance of evil.*

4th DAY: Keys 12, 13, 14. The Life-power in me, and flowing through me does all this. My thoughts, words, and deeds are phases of the Great Transformation. Let me be guided this day by that Messenger of Reality whose office it is to direct my steps along the Way to Freedom. *I am calm and poised amid all these changes, for I know they are transforming me into a perfect image of the One Reality.*

5th DAY: Keys 9, 10, 11. The One Identity watches over me. The cycles of necessity bring me ever nearer to the Inevitable Perfection. Am I in prison? Then I have built its walls myself. Reality needs no walls for its protection, nor will Truth suffer herself to be veiled. *Seeming evil is my opportunity to break down some barriers of ignorance, and find my way into the paradise of things as they are.*

6th Day: Keys 15, 16,17. There are no bondages but that of ignorance and fear. Am I in prison? Then I have built the walls myself. Reality needs no walls for its protection, nor will Truth suffer herself to be veiled. Seeming evil is my opportunity to break down some barriers of ignorance and find my way into the paradise of things as they are.

TAROT INTERPRETATION

Chapter 13

Sure Support

The Tableau for this week is:

10	11	12
13	14	15
16	17	18

The Magic Square is:

13	18	11
12	14	16
17	10	15

The sum of the numbers from 10 to 18 is 126.

In both arrangements, Key 14 (Temperance) is the central picture. The constant summation of the magic square is 42. It shows discrimination (Key 6) as the consequence of the operation of memory (Key 2) through reason (Key 4). Therefore the tableau emphasizes memory as the source where reason draws the material with which it works, so that discrimination may be expressed. Key 14 shows the nature of the process, where we develop discrimination. Key 6 typifies the outcome of this process.

Chapter 12 states that the "Knowledge and Conversation of the Holy Guardian Angel" is your association with a personality a little beyond you on the Way to Freedom.

The messenger who guides you, although they may be only a little more advanced than you, is a messenger or guardian angel. They are a channel to put you in contact with the One Identity.

This week the emphasis is on the process of developing discrimination through correct reasoning using materials provided by memory. Because you are acted upon by intelligences more developed than your own, there comes a time in your occult progress when you realize you are the subject of an experiment.

None of us would have made any progress along the path of attainment had we not been worked upon and experimented with. We are tempered and modified by the loving care of other human beings whose training and experience qualify them for this work. Sometimes it is only after long years that this truth dawns on the student.

We may suppose themselves to be an entirely free agent, doing just exactly what we please. We may pride ourselves on their independence, perseverance, and desire to advance to better things. Sooner or later, we begin to realize that all along, we have been under direction.

As the years pass, we can look back and see how we has been led, gently and lovingly, as the blind are led by those who care for them. With this realization comes a deep humility and thankfulness. One sees then that the protection and care of the One Identity reach us through the channels of other lives. The clearer our consciousness knows this One Identity, the better our angel can act as a director.

We are all at various stages of human development. From those above us, we receive aid, and to some degree, we are the means they employ to carry out their experiments. When we realize this truth, we shall be able to undertake similar tests of our own. As Lao-tze says: "Imperfect men are the materials with which the wise man works."

10 – 14 – 18

This work consists of a series of demonstrations that every human personality is a center of expression for the whole series of cosmic cycles. By our work with those under their direction, the wise learn more and more concerning the Law of Cycles. The effect of our labors makes more conscious of the operation of law.

True occultism is not a system of beliefs. On the contrary, it is a science consisting of verifiable knowledge. The work of a practical occultist aims at the reduction of the number of their *beliefs*, and the establishment in their place *knowledge*.

The subject of the experiments is the occultist's body. The great art is the transformation of one's vehicle. Step by step, it is raised and purified. New cells function, and, at last, the work is completed with the substitution of a deathless, spiritual body - a Master's body from the mortal vehicle with which we were born.

11 – 14 – 17

Such transformations require fine adjustments and demands faith. This faith is the imaginative development, in concrete forms built from a mental substance, of fundamental propositions or seed thoughts that are reasonable and rest on proven facts. The wise admonishes us to test every proposition in the fires of experience. It is not to the lazy that Nature unveils her beauty.

One of the hardest lessons for the beginner of practical occultism is what Jesus expressed by his doctrine of nonresistance. "Reconcile quickly with your accuser while you are going with him to court, lest your accuser hand you over to the judge, and the judge to the guard, and you be put in prison." – Matthew 5:25

For untold millenniums the natural man has regarded every person as a potential enemy and feared nature as an opponent. Ageless Wisdom denies this fallacy. Research demonstrates that nothing in nature is intrinsically hostile to man. Everything has its use. Even the deadliest poisons, understood and applied, is used as a medicine.

Before we may accomplish anything, we must realize our dependence on the cosmic order. We must see that our troubles result from ignorance of the way things are. We must destroy our habits of error by the influx of the light of truth.

13 – 14 – 15

Death must no longer be looked upon as evidence of the unfriendliness of nature. Or regard nature as the power of spiritual evil, malignantly opposing the welfare of humanity. The forces that bring death to a human body can be directed to awaken centers in the brain. These centers can register our experiences during periods when we are functioning on other planes. With this knowledge, we may pass to a higher stage of unfoldment.

In this stage, the adept makes a healthy vehicle that is a channel for the manifestation of the subtle forces of nature. Therefore the adept can exist on the physical plane for years beyond the ordinary life-span. When the adept does lay aside the physical body, it is not death in the usual sense. It is a stoppage of physical function and conscious separation of the higher vehicles of personality from the physical instrument. Therefore, by their ability to remain a long time on the physical plane, an adept has the opportunity to experiment and solve problems requiring lengthy research.

All this begins with the intellectual recognition that every human personality is a particular expression of universal order. At first, this perception is a belief. It is a conviction formed from reasoning and observation of the course of nature. Then comes imaginative development of the seed idea, and the building up of positive mental images. Here all the creative powers of the mind are brought into play.

Since mental images tend to find an outlet in action, the fostering of the seed idea by imagination results in alterations of circumstance, these demonstrations develop faith. Little by little, the old habits of thinking are reversed. There comes into manifestation a corresponding reversal of one's outer situation. Joy takes the place of sorrow, health supplants disease, prosperity replaces poverty, wisdom displaces ignorance.

16 – 17 – 18

This process of verification begins with the overthrow of false ideas.
By substituting accurate observation for superficial acquaintance and
appearances, we build up memories of things as they are, instead of
vague impressions of things as they look. By meditating on what we
have learned, we begin to see relationships unperceived by most
persons. Our meditation affects an adjustment among centers of force
in our bodies.

This represented by the symmetrical arrangement of stars in Key 17.
The stars symbolize forces at work through astral and physical centers
connected with the endocrine glands. Through adjustment of the
functions of these glands, the body chemistry is changed, and we are
transformed from the state of the natural man into the state of spiritual
humanity. The seed of right thought bears fruit in perfected bodies.
By this process, we graduate from the school of natural humanity, to
take our rightful place in the ranks of the "twice-born."

Summary

It cannot be made too emphatic that these methods are directed to effect a physiological modification. Finer vehicles there certainly are, and, as part of our training, we have to learn how to function in them consciously. And how to impress on the physical brain a record of this higher functioning.

Some teaching says the physical body is only an obstacle to spiritual development. This is a gross error. *An unhealthy body is a bar to occult progress.* The wise insist that physical health must precede any attempt to work with finer forces, especially in Yoga, Alchemy, and Magic.

We have learned that even simple and carefully chosen exercises are often misapplied. It seems to be a characteristic of occult immaturity for the pupil to be sure he knows more than his teacher! Even the best efforts of a teacher cannot overcome this tendency. Therefore it becomes necessary to withhold a detailed explanation of technical work until satisfactory evidence of their fitness to receive such instruction. Astral work, in particular, is dangerous for persons who are not healthy.

The main object of occult practice is not the development of the higher vehicles. One of the fallacies of pseudo-occultism is the notion that these vehicles need development. What needs to be purified and perfected is the physical body. Your finer vehicles are all right, just as they are. The Great Work consists of the integration of the "strong force of all forces" here on the physical plane. This work includes various kinds of mental practice. The objective is the building of a new type of organism. The new body will not grow of itself.

Your new body grows by the application of the same laws and forces which have brought it to its present stage of "natural humanity." But it must be taken beyond this stage, and the only way this is done is by conscious, intentional application of these powers to the end that the new creature may be evolved.

Please understand that no work of this kind can succeed if one's efforts are directed to the wrong ends. This is why we insist that the unfoldment of a new type of physical body, rather than the development of finer vehicles, is the object for which we are working.

Since subconsciousness is the body-builder, we shall get our new bodies as a result of its activities. Subconsciousness activities are automatic and are determined by our habitual conscious mental attitudes. The first stages of the Great Work must be those which effect a change in our conscious thinking. It is for this reason that the Tarot series begins with the Magician, which represents the use of our intellectual powers in acts of attention directed to the field of sensory experience. When we observe that field accurately, our minds are stored with correct impressions; it bears fruit in the regeneration of our bodies.

MEDITATIONS

1ˢᵗ DAY: Keys 10, 14, 18. I am on the upward turn of the Wheel of Life, which brings me ever nearer the one Goal. I embrace every opportunity to verify the truths of Ageless Wisdom. The Perfect Law is being built up in my body. *All that I am is related to the whole life expression, and under the guidance of the Universal Mind, I press onward to the heights of liberation.*

2ⁿᵈ DAY; Keys 11, 14, 17. I live my faith. It is a reasonable expectation of eternal progress. Every day I look for fresh revelations of truth. *My whole life is adjusted to the Greater Life that works through me to reveal its perfection.*

3ʳᵈ DAY: Keys 12, 14, 16. I am consciously reversing my former states of mind. I live my life under direction from the One Self. I welcome the overthrow of every erroneous opinion. *I am the unmoved witness of the great transmutation. It puts an end to the sense of separateness.*

4th DAY: Keys 13, 14, 15. I welcome change. I see in all experience that the One Life works upon me to purify my personality. I face problems with patience, for I am one with That which knows the right answers to them all. *This is a new day, and I meet its tests with joy, confident that every seeming adversary is but another opportunity.*

5th DAY: Keys 10, 11, 12. The Spirit at the heart of the universe is one with my spirit. The law which rules the stars rules also in my members. My support is in the Eternal. *I am unmoved by changing circumstances, poised amid action, confident of support through all apparent vicissitudes.*

6th DAY: Keys 16, 17, 18. This day the lightning-flash of some new knowledge of Reality rids me of another error. Let me he still, that I may see the truth. The path is open before me, and I press onward toward the goal. *I am free from the sense of separateness. I rest this day in the unbroken knowledge that even in my body, I am being raised to a height beyond all former attainments.*

TAROT INTERPRETATION

Chapter 14

Renewing the Mind

The Tableau for this week is:

11	12	13
14	15	16
17	18	19

The Magic Square is:

14	19	12
13	15	17
18	11	16

The sum of the numbers from 11 to 16 is 135.

In both arrangements, the central Key is number 15, the Devil. The constant summation of the magic square is 45. It shows our consciousness of the overshadowing presence of the One Identity (Key 9) as the consequence of the operation of intuition (Key 5) through reason (Key 4). The tableau shows intuition as the source of material upon which reason works, so that we may become responsive to the One Identity. Key 15 shows what brings us to this awareness. Key 9 is the representation of that awareness.

It is also noteworthy that the constant summation of the magic square is the number of Adam (אדם).

ם	ד	א
40	4	1

This square of Tarot Keys yields an answer to the question, "What is humanity?" Also, 45 is the theosophic extension of 9. That means 45 is the sum of 0 to 9 $(1 + 2 + 3 + 4 + 5 + 6 + 7 + 8 + 9 = 45)$. Therefore 45 symbolizes the complete expression of the power represented by Key 9.

If we put all these ideas together, Tarot is reminding us:

1. That reason is not limited to experience, or the senses, or materials. It may receive material from above its level, and when higher knowledge comes down, it must be fitted into our reasoned constitution of the universe. It is also true of anything learned from observation, called from memory, or suggested by imagination. The Emperor does not surrender his rule at his level, even to the Hierophant. Reason must check up on intuition before intuition can be of use. Intuition (5) is above reason (4), but never contrary to reason.

2. Awareness of the One Identity comes to us intuitively. However, this intuition is not complete realization. To attain realization, the intuition must be perceived at the conscious level of reason. This is necessary because the full understanding of our relation to the One Identity requires changes in our bodily structure and chemistry.

The natural man cannot receive the higher knowledge of the Spirit. The bodily changes are made by subconsciousness that enables us to receive that knowledge. The subconscious mind is under the direction of the self-consciousness. Key 6 suggests that we may train subconsciousness that she will act as the reflector of superconscious knowledge into our field of personal awareness. To give us a full realization, subconsciousness must change our physical bodies. She cannot perform this work until our observations lead us to the reasoned conclusion of the powers of subconsciousness.

This is the inner significance of that passage which says:

"Therefore, I urge you, brothers and sisters, because of God's mercy, to offer your bodies as a living sacrifice, holy and pleasing to God – this is your true and proper worship. Do not conform to the pattern of this world, but be transformed by the renewing of your mind. Then you will be able to test and approve what God's will is – his good, pleasing, and perfect will." – Romans 12: 1 & 2.

Recall that Key 9 represents the Intelligence of Will.

3. That the place of humanity in the cosmic order is to act as an agent whereby the Cosmic Will may be proved or tested and tried. Humanity is ready for a transformation. Evolution cannot carry us any farther along the path. A thousand generations hence will find no human liberated from conformity to "this world," unless they participate in their self-evolution. The unique position of humanity is that we can change our bodies by changing our minds. Therefore we have a new instrument through which the Life-power may manifest the higher levels of its potencies.

Faith is required in the Great Work. Key 11, which represents the Faithful Intelligence, shows us that this is not blind faith. The properly instructed student of Ageless Wisdom has a deep and abiding faith, rooted in observation, and perfected by reason. The problems of life do not look less terrifying to an occultist than they do to an ordinary person. The difference is that the practical occultist has been through a course of training which makes them know that no problem is as bad as it looks.

As we advance in our experimental work, we learn there are sources of knowledge and power other than those reported to us by our senses. We are not sense-bound. When we begin to succeed in practical work, we become a new creature.

Our outward appearance isn't different from the rest of humanity. Our inner life is of a different kind. We know ourselves to belong to a virtual new species – self-generated.

In the passage Romans, the original Greek says: "Be not fashioned by this age." Such is the invariable message of Ageless Wisdom. Therefore are its adepts like strangers, even among their kin, men and women whose whole course of life is looked upon with distrust. Adepts conceal their aims and convictions because they are often denounced and persecuted, even unto death. What is the fashion at any age is never the Inner Truth, for fashions change under the influence of the race subconsciousness.

The practical occultist aims to reverse conditions by reversing their thoughts. Their views are in nearly the exact opposites of those held by the natural man.

For example, Eliphas Levi, says of the Great Magical Agent: "The Astral Light is the key of all dominion. It is the first physical manifestation of the Divine Breath. The Gnostics represented it as the burning body of the Holy Ghost. It is represented on ancient monuments by the serpent devouring its tail. It is the Hyle of the Gnostics. Lastly, it is the devil of exoteric dogmatism."

That is, what Tarot represents by Key 15. But what a reversal of popular opinion to say that the "key of all dominion" is the "devil of exoteric dogmatism." Small wonder that sages have suffered martyrdom in every age when the herd mentality has had the upper hand in the affairs of men!

The problem the practical occultist faces is one that has varied and ever-shifting forms. It is a problem of ignorance as to the reversal of the currents of the Astral Light. Those who solve this problem can rule all things. They can change their physical body that it may be used as an instrument for the direction of modes of force which would consume the ordinary physical vehicle.

"Dissolution is the secret of the Great Work." Alchemist represents dissolution by the symbol, which you see on Key 10, just above the letter R on the wheel. This is also the symbol for the Aquarius (♒), the Water-bearer. Aquarius is the sign which has the greatest power in the age we are entering. It is peculiarly a human sign represented on Keys 10 and 21 by the man's head at the upper left-hand corner of the design.

The Fool looks towards the Aquarius sign. In chemistry, dissolution is called analysis. Every problem has first to be analyzed. Its parts must be separated from one another and carefully measured.

In Key 15, we see pictured many parts, put together in a disorderly, chaotic fashion. To understand the picture of the Devil, we take it to pieces. Then we see that it represents something both male and female. It is something found in all the elements (wings= Air; eagle's talons = Water; goat's horns & gross body = Earth; torch = Fire). The whole design represents a disorderly combination of forces, and the reversed pentagram at the top of the picture gives a clue to the cause of the confusion. Trouble comes whenever man's ignorance reverses his position of dominion over the elements.

In general, every problem is a phase of what Key 15 symbolizes. Analysis of any problem into its parts is valuable because it shows where these parts fit into the cosmic order. Thus investigation leads to synthesis, and synthesis unveils the beautiful truth behind the ugly face of every problem.

14 – 15 – 16

Humans must participate in their self-evolution if they are to advance to higher levels than the herd-mind. Ageless Wisdom teaches that humans have no power which they may contribute to the Great Work, or may, if they so determine, withhold from that Work. Then humans would be more powerful than the Universal Spirit whence we came and could defeat the purposes of Spirit. It is not until Spirit works upon us, from within and without, has changed us so that we realize what is going on within us that we participate in the Great Work.

Paul wrote: "The natural man does not accept the things that come from the Spirit of God. For they are foolishness to him, and he cannot understand them, because they are spiritually discerned." – 1 Corinthians 2:14

Up to a certain point, we are all subjects of the transmutation process. Beyond a point, we become participants. From then on, there is a subtle but significant change in our mental attitude. We no longer fear problems. We welcome every challenge as a fresh opportunity.

Problems do not look any less terrifying, but they cease to daunt us. We know ourselves to be centers of expression for a power wise enough to resolve every problem into its parts and bring those parts together again in an orderly arrangement. We face every problem boldly, without bitterness of heart.

This state of mind does not come all at once. It is preceded by the break-up of many structures of false knowledge. Storm and stress precede the calm of serene meditation. The book of Psalms says that a heart shattered and broken is not despised by God. We must dissolve our subconscious complexes of erroneous opinion, based on the illusion of separateness as being. There is no advancing beyond the stage of bondage to problems and circumstances. This stage of extreme discomfort is the ordinary predicament of the natural man.

Transformation begins with faith. Please understand, faith is not limited to religion, philosophy, or metaphysics. Scientists exercise a degree of faith that surpasses anything by the religious devotee. No person ever saw an electron or a gene, but few scientists doubt their existence. The fission of the atom was accomplished by men who had faith in things unseen, which were revealed to them by the symbols of pure mathematics.

Dr. George Crile asserted that in a cubic inch of our muscles, there are four billion tiny points of radiant energy. Each point has a temperature from 3,000 to 6,000 degrees centigrade. His faith in the presence of these tiny hot points in our bodies is a reasonable faith, justified by the fact that living tissue emits ultra-violet rays. Dr. Crile argues that it takes a temperature of at least 3,000 degrees to produce ultra-violet rays. Therefore these high temperatures must be extremely tiny hot points our muscles. We do not feel the heat because the points are so tiny that they do not affect our senses.

The advance of science confirms the ancient doctrines and strengthens our reasonable conviction that human life is related to, and is dependent on, the entire world-organism. The whole universe flows through us, and the stuff from which our bodies are made is structurally a miniature copy of the stars of heaven.

The fiery energy is the basis of our existence as human personalities. The particular form of it which holds greatest possibilities for us is that which usually finds expression through the reproductive function.

When we know the nature of this energy, we can control its currents, and reverse their ordinary operation. By this means we emerge from the bondage of the natural man into the freedom of the higher order of being for which the natural man is but a seed-form. In so emerging from natural humanity, we shall be released as our final demonstration, from bondage to the appearance of death, which the Bible describes as the "last enemy."

Meditation is an essential practice involved in our release from natural humanity. It is a state of intentional receptivity to the spiritual life which flows into our field of personality from superconscious levels. We must open ourselves to that life to meditate. However, we must keep self-consciousness on the alert, and direct our attention to a specific object toward or around which, the stream of intelligence coming from higher levels may be made to flow. Right meditation should always be aimed at the coordination of all our energies, as hinted by the balanced arrangement of stars in Key 17.

Meditation changes the physical body, alters its chemistry and structure. Our emergence from the state of natural humanity is as a physiological adaptation, as is the development of the natural man from the animal kingdom. The transformation by the renewing of our minds is an actual regeneration. This transformation is what the wise mean by the statement, "we must be born again."

MEDITATIONS

1st DAY: 11, 15, 19. Today I have fresh opportunities to adjust and adapt the forces of life. These opportunities come as the problems I shall meet this day. Through solving them, I may become a new creature. *I have the power to adjust all difficulties, for I am a direct expression of the ruling power of the universe.*

2nd DAY: 12, 15, 18. Today I set myself to reverse my former errors. Let me remember that whatever frightens me does so because I have not learned its meaning. Let me press onward in the Way of Liberation, toward the goal of enlightenment. *I am an agent of the Spirit of Life, which knows the answers to all my problems and is shaping my very flesh to the end that I may solve them.*

3rd DAY: 13, 15, 17. I am transformed by the renewing of my mind. There is no bondage for me, save that of my ignorance. That bondage I dissolve today through calm meditation. *I analyze my problems and discern the opportunities they hold for me, through my steady meditation on their true meaning.*

4th DAY: 14, 15, 16. I see myself today as the subject of the Great Work of spiritual transmutation. My bondage, however real it may appear, is only delusion. It will end when I am released from the prison of error I have built. *The One Self is working through me to solve every problem and release me from all erroneous opinions.*

5th DAY: 11, 12, 13. My faith is grounded in reason. I entrust myself to a cosmic order for which I have abundant evidence. Not even death frightens me, for I know its benevolent purpose. *I am poised and secure in the midst of change.*

6th DAY: 17, 18, 19. Today, in silent meditation, I shall catch a new glimpse of truth, for I am being transformed bodily by the new knowledge I am receiving. The process of regeneration is at work within me. *As I see the truth, I am transformed into a perfect likeness of my spiritual origin.*

TAROT INTERPRETATION

Chapter 15

Inspiration

The Tableau for this week is:

12	13	14
15	16	17
18	19	20

The Magic Square is:

15	20	13
14	16	18
19	12	17

The sum of the numbers from 12 to 17 is 144.

In both arrangements, the central card is Key 16, the Tower. The constant summation of the magic square is 48. It shows the adept's reversal of normal states of consciousness (Key 12) as the result of the working of the law represented by Key 8 through reason (Key 4).

This tableau shows that to reason correctly, we must use the law that all subhuman states of the life-force are under the control of the human subconsciousness. The faulty reasoning is often the result of our ignorance of this law. Key 16 shows the state of consciousness which is the result of our release from complexes of mistaken opinion.

Forty-eight is also the number of Kokab (כוכב) – the planet Mercury. It relates to the power of attentive concentration pictured in the Tarot by the Magician.

כ	ו	כ	ב
20	6	20	2

Kokab also means "star." The Great Magical Agent, or Astral Light, is (אור הכוכבים), Aur ha-Kokabim – Light of the Stars. The enumeration of these two words is 310, and this is the number of דוש, to conquer, חבש, to bind, and יש, essence, being.

Levi says The Astral Light is the blind force souls must conquer. It binds us as long as we remain in ignorance of its nature and laws. It is the material basis of our being, for it is the substance of heaven and earth, diffused throughout infinity. When we master and direct its currents, we become depositaries of the power of God. The Astral Light, the First Matter of the alchemists. It is the superconscious power represented by Key 0. The self-conscious modes of expression are symbolized by Key 1, and whose subconscious law of operation is pictured by Key 2. Note that 310 is also the number of כפיר, a young lion (see Key 8).

The central idea of this tableau is represented by Key 16. It is the overthrow of error by right knowledge. Your studies of Key 16 say the basis of error is the delusion of separateness, pictured by the lonely peak on which the Tower is built. Right knowledge is symbolized by the lightning-flash, which is also a symbol of the flaming sword, representing the ten Sephiroth.

In Hebrew the flaming sword (Genesis 3:24) is להט החרב *lawhat ha-khreb* (44 + 215 = 259). *Lawhat* is translated *flaming*, also means *magical*, or "the force of enchantment." By number, it is connected with the noun *dam* (דם), blood. *Ha-khereb*, the sword, is equal by numeration to (ארוה), a path, a narrow way, and to (זרה), to irradiate, to rise (as the sun).

Briefly stated, the magical force is in the blood. To direct it is to find liberation, and as it rises in our consciousness and sends its radiance through our lives, we are set free.

It is called the flaming sword in the story of the fall of humanity. Genesis has an allegory of the descent of consciousness from the higher and inner planes to the physical. The sword turns every way because it is the fire force in the bloodstream, circulating through our bodies, and therefore turning in every direction. It keeps us out of Eden, for the time being, so that we may gain knowledge of the physical plane.

12 – 16 – 19

The force in our blood is what we learn to use to overcome the delusions, which cause our difficulties. To break up our complexes of error, represented by the Tower, we must adopt the mental attitude expressed by Key 12. Conscious and voluntary reversal of our thinking is indispensable. This reversal must be practiced continually.

We must reverse the notion that we are separate beings. We must reverse the idea that we are personally independent. We are related mentally and spiritually to the cosmic whole, and dependent thereon (Holographic Universe). We must also reverse our idea of the pronoun "I." It's not singular but plural. Our identity is linked with the One Identity – as is everyone else.

This takes a lot of practice, and it does not come naturally. Eventually, the practice will overthrow our subconscious complexes of error. It works on our physical bodies by changing them a little every day. This practice alters chemistry and structure until, at last, we are released from bondage to three-dimensional appearances. We come to know ourselves as four-dimensional beings. Remember, we do not become four-dimensional beings by this practice. When we become directly aware that we are four-dimensional beings, then we can exercise powers belonging to that state.

The Mars force is involved in the transformation of personality, which overthrows error. The magic power is flaming in our bloodstream and every cell. The magic flame flows out of the symbolic North, the place of darkness and terror, which represents all things unknown, toward the East and South, representing enlightenment and power. It is by control of forces that inspire terror, and surrounded with taboos, that the real magician, transforms themselves, and then, through themselves, the world.

The magician works first upon themselves, so they may build a new organism, capable of registering vibrations in the environment which pass unperceived. The new organism can direct forces which an ordinary human body cannot manipulate. The magician finds themselves in a new world, ordered in ways that seem miraculous to ignorant. We deny and destroy the old "self," for that false self is nonexistent. *Thus all magic includes self-immolation.*

Out of the destroyed false self, sacrificed on the flaming pyre of knowledge, rises, like the Phoenix, the true Self. This regenerated Self is the solar being whose instruments are the transmuted self-consciousness and subconsciousness that are identified with the *great Intelligence whose physical brain is the Sun*. There's a real occult statement for you. It says much in few words. May you extract from it its full meaning.

This same Sun-Spirit is the Holy Guardian Angel pictured in Key 14. Fortunately for us, we do not have to perform the Great Work with no more than the meager equipment afforded by our consciousness. The individual consciousness is worked upon, and at one stage of the work, it is completely broken up, in order that it may be reconstituted. Notice that the lightning-flash in Key 16 comes from outside the Tower, and springs from a solar disc.

Adepts who are close to the final realization say with St. Paul, "l die daily." They are conscious of the dissolution of the persons they used to be and rejoice. In alchemy, this stage of the Great Work is called putrefaction. It is the disorganization of the combinations which entered into the make-up of the old personality. Refusal to enter into this stage of the Great Work keeps many students from making a practical demonstration. Remember, you cannot stay as you are and become an adept. The path is a path of reorganization, and to gain the crown at its end, you must pass far beyond the states and conditions of ordinary human personality.

What problem confronts you now? That is your starting point. Try to realize that the real nature of that problem is this: you are mistaken about something. What you are ignorant of, primarily, is some aspect of your authentic power. There is power enough to enable you to meet that problem. There is wisdom sufficient to correct your error. Nothing will help you, so long as you hang onto the error. This problem you face is no exception to the general perfection of the cosmic order. It is an opportunity for you to get rid of some pet bit of nonsense you are treasuring. Few people like to be told this, but the few who have ears to hear are the ones who eventually become adepts and masters.

The typical reaction to a problem is either to run away, blame somebody else, or the stars, or Fate, or Karma. The unusual response to a problem is to see in it an opportunity for the unveiling of some hitherto unrecognized aspect of truth.

Have you heard of "The Dweller on the Threshold" perhaps? The "Dweller" is none other than your false self. On what threshold does he stand? On the threshold of the Adytum of "god-nourished silence." On the threshold of the Gate of Eden. Remember that *paradise* means *an enclosure*. The path of liberation leads within. The powers which release us are within. The beautiful pleasure garden where nature unveils herself is also within. What more, need be said?

Reverse the ordinary attitudes of humanity, and you attain to the consciousness of the adept. You do not become anything that you are not now. This is a strange doctrine, but true. You do not become, but you do enter into a new region of knowledge. You do not add to yourself anything. *You find what you already possess.* Franklin, Galvani, Faraday, and Edison did not bring electricity into the world. Their knowledge of it was the seed of this electrical age.

Reverse ordinary states of human consciousness, and you die to the personality that you were while those states dominated your mind. You die, but in dying, you learn that there is no death, and find yourself liberated from the notion that you must have a physical body to be alive.

Those experiences which abolish the consciousness of death come relatively early on the path of liberation. Reverse the false appearances of "this world," and you find that the Knowledge and Conversation of the Holy Guardian Angel is Self-knowledge.

Can we be plainer? How many will hear and understand? The *Fama Fraternitatis* says, "that man might thereby understand his nobleness and worth, and why he is called Microcosms, and how far his knowledge extended into Nature."

The Life-power has to be incorporated in an organism before its higher manifestations are expressed on the physical plane. This is the occult truth behind the doctrines of incarnation. This is the hidden mystery of "the Word made flesh." The natural man has a natural body. The adept has an adept's body. The body you have now is the seed from which you develop a higher organism, but you must participate consciously in the development. The actual building of your new body is accomplished at subconscious levels, symbolized by the Moon above the path in Key 18.

The way or method, whereby this is accomplished, is the middle way between the extremes of artificiality and the general averages of nature. This method leads to regeneration.

Regeneration is not a metaphysical term. It designates a generative process, occurring in the occultist's physical body. As a result, we develop an organ for the solar consciousness mentioned in this chapter. Then our personal conscious and subconscious life is renewed, and we become as a little child. From this regeneration, we pass on to the next stage of unfoldment, in which ordinary restrictions of time and space do not affect the adept's action.

Summary

This is not so far off in the future, as you may suppose. Doctrines which pretend that this realization is far off are false. If we mentality grasps the principle, we have arrived at the stage where a considerable measure of realization is possible. This message is not sent you as a promise to be fulfilled some twenty incarnations hence, nor in some after-life to which death is the portal.

It is a message of hope for the here and now, intended to rouse your expectation of better conditions in this life. *You are a four-dimensional being.* You are not bound by the limits of space and time. Your effective range is far beyond what most persons suppose.

Right now, you can, and do, heal or hurt at a distance, and your activity affects the lives of others who may live thousands of miles away. These teachings aim to accomplish is to awaken men and women to clear understanding of what they are. You must know what you are doing before you can do it intelligently.

It may seem to you that we set the mark too high. Not so. The world needs healers and thinkers who can consciously project their constructive imagery into mental space. Many are called, and if few are chosen, it is because only a few understand what it is, and fewer still are working.

MEDITATIONS

1st DAY: Keys 12, 16, 20. The movement of universal forces is the basis of all my activities. Let me be free from the delusion of separateness. Let me be free from the belief that I am bound by time and space. *Doing nothing of myself, I yet enter freely into all activity, for my real life is the Universal Life.*

2nd DAY: Keys 13, 16, 19. All things are made new for me this day. The errors of the past cannot imprison me. Today, I am a new creature. *The seed of the new life springs within me into its unfoldment, breaking down all barriers and uniting me consciously to the radiance of my shining Self.*

3rd DAY: Keys 14, 16, 18. My consciousness is being transmuted by my true Self. Its inspiration shatters the delusion, which is the only bondage. In my flesh, the flaming magic sword turns every way to cut off all that is false. *The alchemy of Spirit transmutes my bondage into freedom, and I press onward to the goal of perfect realization.*

4th DAY: Keys 15, 16, 17. I rejoice in this day's problems. They are opportunities to break down the walls of ignorance. I watch expectantly for the unveiling of truth. *My problem is an opportunity to overcome errors and see the beauty that is.*

5th DAY: Keys 12, 13, 14. The more I yield to the One Life, the more it yields itself to me. What I was dies out as what I am becoming ever clearer. I am guided safely through this day. *Supported by the One Great Life, through all appearances of change, all my forces are adjusted by the One Self.*

6th DAY: Keys 18, 19, 20. My subconsciousness is continually at work to build a finer body. In that body is awakening the new life of the spiritual man that I truly am. I am set free from every limitation. *My body is regenerated into the divine likeness, which knows no bondage of time or space.*

TAROT INTERPRETATION

Chapter 16

Isis Unveiled

The Tableau for this lesson is

13	14	15
16	17	18
19	20	21

The Magic Square is

16	21	14
15	17	19
20	13	18

$16 + 21 + 14 = 51$.
$15 + 17 + 19 = 51$.
$20 + 13 + 18 = 51$.

The sum of the numbers from 13 to 21 is 153.

Central in both arrangements is Key 17, the Star. The constant summation of the magic square is 51. It shows discrimination (Key 6) as the manifestation of attentive observation (Key 1) through intuition (Key 5). This tableau emphasizes the representation, attention, concentration, and all else that the Magician symbolizes concerning discrimination. What is pictured in Key 6 is the outcome of intuition, but intuition does not work unless observation at self-conscious levels has been called into play. Intuition supplies what self-conscious reasoning and observation cannot give — however, intuition requires that self-conscious reasoning and observation to provide the mind with materials to work on. We arrange the elements of life at self-conscious levels, as the Magician arranges his implements on the table. When the arrangement is finished, the Hierophant gives us its meaning. *No meaning is given until the arrangement is made.*

Note that the number 51 is three times 17, the number of the Key at the center of the magic square. This holds for the central Keys of all the magic squares in this series. Their constant summation is always three times the number printed on the primary Key.

The arrangement points to the operation represented by the central Key, at the three levels of superconsciousness, self-consciousness, and subconsciousness. In the nine-fold arrangement,

1. The upper row of Keys represents superconscious manifestations.
2. The middle row stands for self-conscious manifestations.
3. The bottom row symbolizes the subconscious manifestations of the powers represented by the Keys.

The main idea of this tableau is that Nature unveils herself. We do not unveil her. The veil hiding Isis is our ignorance; even this is lifted by Isis. Nature is the power of Spirit, "the mysterious power, difficult to cross over." Nature is Spirit in action, and our quest for reality is another phase of that same action. Spirit is the actual Self. In us, it works to bring about the changes in our vehicles, which constitute our enlightenment. You who read this lesson read it because Spirit, your real Self, has brought you to this present stage of the Great Work, Spirit speaks to you through these words. These lessons are a means whereby the true I AM makes itself known to you.

$$13 - 17 - 21$$

Eliphas Levi says, "Death has no existence in the Sanctum Regnum of existence. A change, however, awful demonstrates movement, and movement is life: only those who have attempted to check the disrobing of the spirit have tried to create a real death. We are all dying and being renewed every day because every day, our bodies have changed to some extent. Understand well that the life-current of the progress of souls is regulated by a law of development which carries the individual ever upward."

By dying and renewal, the truth becomes manifest. We must be receptive if we would learn the inner doctrine. We cannot be responsive until we have rid ourselves of false personalities. When we know how to redirect and sublimate the currents of the Great Magical Agent, which brings death until we subdue it, we can participate in the higher consciousness pictured by Key 21.

14 – 17 – 20

One observance needs to be insisted on — the tempering all activities through the exercise of their opposites. Levi has words of wisdom. "If you desire a long life and health, avoid all excesses, carry nothing to extremes. So when you have passed beyond the mortal sphere by the allurements of ecstasy, return to yourself, seek repose, and enjoy the pleasures which life supplies for the wise, but do not indulge yourself too freely. Let there be no misunderstanding. To vanquish an enemy, there must be no running away. True victory can only follow meeting him face to face, joining in a struggle, and so showing your command over him."

Only a balanced person can be a practical occultist. Only a balanced person, thoroughly poised in mind, emotions, and body, may look without peril on the face of truth. Consider well the balanced disposition of the stars in Key 17.

To enter into the realization of your fourth-dimensional nature, you must achieve equilibrium between the conscious and subconscious elements of your mind. Then from that equilibrium spring, a new awareness of the meaning of personality (typified by the child in Key 20). In that awareness, you know yourself as free from time, space, and all forms of bondage growing out of these illusions.

15 – 17 – 19

Most people fear problems and difficulties. The terrors of the unknown have filled the race mind with a host of dreadful images whose name truly is "Legion." They have no substance other than the mind-stuff fashioned by humanities' ignorant fears. Potent they are, while we fear and believe in them. Like pursuers in a nightmare, they approach ever nearer to us, however fast we run away. We must turn and face them boldly. Examine a problem carefully and concentrate intensely upon it. Then meditation will reveal its real significance and present you with a solution. Always in such solutions, you will find means to further your regeneration. Invariably they show a way to transmute some part of your old personality into a better likeness of your essential divinity.

16 – 17 – 18

In Key 16 there are 22 Yods (ʾ) are shown in two groups. At the right of the tower are ten, arranged in the Tree of Life. At the left of the tower, twelve are drawn to suggest two circles, one above the other, like a figure 8. The tower is built on an isolated peak (rook). Its twenty-two courses are of white brick, a symbol of the "moonshine" of personal opinion.

None of the powers that make-up your existence is dependent on material manifestation. They support themselves, and like the Yods, they are floating in free space. An error of errors is this belief in the importance of form – the dependence on things. Immaterial forces project themselves into our material existence (including our bodies and physical environment). Things are the external manifestation of invisible and internal realities.

Therefore the kneeling woman in Key 17 is nude, in contrast to the garmented figures falling from the tower. The symbolism of Key 17 is a picture of smooth, fluidic motion, in contrast to the apparent stability of the tower and its rocky base. What holds us back from progress is our desire to preserve forms of existence we have enjoyed.

At the bottom of the path in Key 18 is a hard-shelled animal. Further, up the path are the soft-skinned dog and wolf. In the middle distance are towers representing the works of humans. Between them is an opening, and the Way of Return leads far beyond the towers – far beyond structure and protection of form. Key 18 refers to the gradual unfoldment of the powers within us that changes our bodies so that they become less and less dense. Finally, in adeptship, we reach a stage where our body structure is altered so that it is relatively easy to disintegrate them. This is accomplished by raising their vibrations from the physical plane to higher octaves of manifestation. Only those who are free from bondage to form and structure attain the greatest heights of adeptship.

Think about death until you see the death of physical bodies is a benevolent provision of Nature. While we fear death, we cannot master the forces that will free us from death. To study anything close enough to discover its secret is impossible, so long as one fears it. We must change our train our consciousness to focus on the One-Power that governs the projection of forms into time and space.

When we become sufficiently aware of the Transmuter, the real Self, then we are aware that our being is one with that Eternal Being. Then we welcome problems. However, terrifying the face of circumstance, we know that dwelling within us is the Lord of Circumstance. Those who are consciously aware of the true nature of the Self are preserved by that knowledge from evil.

The regenerated human has a solar consciousness. Other schools speak of a solar body, but the two statements are one. There is a danger of misinterpretation. We do not identify ourselves with a being whose organism is our solar system (Horus the Elder). Instead, we identify with the One Being whose body is the entire universe.

We progress in stages, and one of those stages is identifying the Self as the Solar Logos whose brain is the Sun, and the body is the rest of our solar system. However, we do not stop here.

We arrive at a stage of realization, so we receive impulses of superconscious (the white sun of The Fool) relayed to us from the solar brain (Key 19). When this awareness is perfected, we function as immediate expressions of the Solar Intelligence and share its perfect fourth-dimensional awareness.

The natural man cannot act as an instrument for the Solar Intelligence, because the organ of awareness is not yet developed. This organ is the single eye to which Jesus referred in his cryptic statement, "Your eye is like a lamp that provides light for your body. When your eye is healthy, your whole body is filled with light." (Matthew 6:22) This is not a metaphor. The pineal gland is the eye, and when it is in full development, it gives us a new vision. In that order of vision, one outstanding feature is the direct perception of the absolute unity of existence.

Ordinary sight is concerned with light and shade, with many pairs of opposites. The solar consciousness sees unity. The man or woman who has developed the single eye has a body capable of receiving the vibrations of the solar consciousness, thereby freed from the influence of all the pairs of opposites.

Ordinarily, we think of ourselves as beings, and of the universe as something in contrast to ourselves. We see the universe as a vast number of things. The Spiritual Knower perceives the universe as ONE and identifies themselves as that ONE. There remains no trace of otherness in their consciousness.

Identification begins as an intellectual classification. Before the full glory of the experience may come to us, we have to perceive our rightful place in the cosmic order. This intelligent identification is an act of reason and results in faith. The faith then becomes a potent suggestion, which acts on subconsciousness so that our bodies are regenerated. Then the third eye opens, and we perceive the full splendor of our real nature. We find no words for this, nor shall we waste time in a vain attempt to describe this transcendent experience. This first-hand knowledge of reality is not far off for any reader who will dedicate themselves to the work of becoming ripe.

MEDITATIONS

1st DAY: Keys 13, 17, 21. The person I was, even a moment ago, is no more, for the form of my existence is undergoing ceaseless modifications. The truth I see today was hidden from me yesterday by the form assumed yesterday by my consciousness. The perfect realization toward which I move will find me even more transformed.

As I change, the truth becomes clearer to me, and at last, I shall achieve perfect identification with Universal Spirit.

2nd DAY: Keys 14, 17, 20. Let me be free this day from the influence of the pairs of opposites. Truth is ONE, and not TWO. I am a center of expression for the ONE BEING, which is, in every moment, free from the duality of time and space.

The real Self equilibrates all my activities, reveals truth to me and sets me free from mortality.

3rd DAY: 15, 17, 19. My real Self solves all problems. The solutions reveal the truth to me. Answers come from sources outside the limitations of my sensory awareness.

I welcome problems, because they are new opportunities to see truth, and to make manifest powers beyond those affecting my physical senses.

4th DAY: Keys 16, 17, 18. My existence is the expression of forces having no material basis. My personality is not a form but a flux. My body is an evolving instrument, being made ever finer for the uses of the Self.

I rely on spirit, not on form, on movement, not on structure; even in my physical body I am changing daily into a more responsive instrument of the Life-Power.

5th DAY: Keys 13, 14, 15, I cannot die, because I never was born. This incarnation of mine is but one of many stages of the Great Work. The only evil consists in the belief that one can stand still.

I welcome every change. I know that my true self is shaping my personality day by day into a means more adequate for the solution of every problem.

6th DAY: Keys 19, 20, 21. This personality of mine is even now experiencing the mental and physical transmutations which bring about regeneration. I am already a fourth dimensional immortal, not a three-dimensional mortal. My true Self is a Single Identity animating the whole universe.

Today I am a new creature, awakened from the nightmare of mortality, consciously one with the spiritual reality of all things.

Tarot Interpretations

Chapter 17

Jupiter Magic Square and the
1st Stage of Spiritual Unfoldment

The Tarot Magic Square for this chapter is,

3	13	14	0
8	6	5	11
4	10	9	7
15	1	2	12

3 + 13 + 14 + 0 = 30
8 + 6 + 5 + 11 = 30
4 + 10 + 9 + 7 = 30
15 + 1 + 2 + 12 = 30

The summation of the numbers 0 to 15 is 120.

Layout the Keys as above. Inspect the tableau before reading the lesson. The combinations are different from those to which you are accustomed. Let your subconsciousness receive the impression of the whole tableau. Before reading further, see what you can discover concerning its details.

This is the first of seven lessons on the Jupiter magic squares. It is a symmetrical arrangement of numbers, from which is derived a magical figure called the Sigil of Jupiter.

The sigil is made by connecting the central points of the sixteen cells of a Jupiter square. The center of the square numbered 0 is the beginning and end of the line forming the sigil. Straight lines connect the centers of the cells, in the order of the numbers from 0 to 15. The resultant figure is shown below. In ceremonial and talismanic magic, this figure is employed in the operations of Jupiter. It is drawn with violet ink, paint, or crayon.

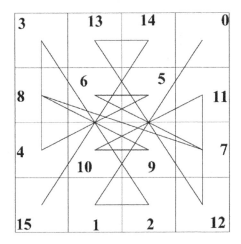

There are other magic squares of sixteen numbers, but this particular arrangement has been handed down to us as having special potency in Jupiter operations. Its harmonious character, considered as a balanced system of lines.

In these Jupiter squares, note the diagonals, 3 – 6 – 9 – 12 and 0 – 5 – 10 – 15. 0 and 10 are balanced by 5, and 5 and 15 are balanced by 10. On the other diagonal 3 and 9 are balanced by 6, while 6 and 12 are balanced by 9.

The 1st Stage of Spiritual Unfoldment – Bondage

The sum of any two numbers opposed, as 0 + 15, 1 + 14, 4 + 11, or 7 + 8, is 15. Therefore the *square corresponds to the first stage of spiritual unfoldment, represented by Key 15.* This square has to do with the initial recognition of bondage, the facing of a problem. It is also connected with the 26th Path on the Tree of Life, The Renewing Intelligence.

In the meditations for this lesson, and the next six, the fundamental ideas are taken from the four horizontal and two diagonal rows of Keys — also the ideas suggested by the letters corresponding to the Keys. The horizontal rows, like Hebrew, is read right to the left. The diagonal row from upper right to lower left is read from bottom to top, and the other diagonal is read from the upper left to the lower right.

0 – 14 – 13 – 3

"I utter myself by seeing," says The Book of Tokens. The Heavenly Vision is the real cause of the Earthly Appearance. This physical universe is the embodiment of the mental seeing which is a quality of the Scintillating Intelligence, pictured by the Tarot Fool. Not yet do we share that vision, because it is beyond at a level which to us is superconscious. However, the wise say the Spirit of Life in us is now, and always the Seer of that glorious Beyond that reaches inconceivable heights (Key 0). The Seer is with us always. It is the genius represented by Key 14. From it, we derive all our aspirations. From it comes the impulse and power to advance. The One Seer is the One Actor also, and from that One's action all our deeds are derived (Key 14).

This One is the dissolver of all delusion. Steadily it moves in its progress from the darkness of the Unknown toward the sunlight of the perfect manifestation. Endlessly it reaps the fruit of the past in the field of the present. To the unwise, it wears the horrible aspect of death, but it is the Great Harvester is the Sower of the New Day in another guise (Key 13).

From the seeds sown springs up the rich ideas and forms suggested by the ripening grain at the feet of the Empress. Daleth (ד), a symbol of the womb, follows Nun (נ), which represents the Martian, phallic, and masculine power.

The first row in the magic square above ends with Key 3 corresponding to Venus. It relates to the creative function of subconsciousness. Vision, experiment, action, and the formulation of new mental patterns are suggested by this series of Keys. The planetary sequence is,

1. Iconoclastic Uranus (0).

2. The expansive and orderly Jupiter (14 – Sagittarius ruled by Jupiter).

3. The transforming and disintegrating Mars (16 - Scorpio – ruled by Jupiter).

4. The formative and integrating Venus (3).

11 – 5 – 6 – 8

The conjoined powers of Venus and Saturn are represented by the Key (11). Equilibrium is always the basis of the work of the practical occultist. We do not seek to escape from the order of the universe. Never do we try to evade it. Practical occultism is living the law in strict conformity to the way things are. This requires imagination (Venus) and concrete embodiment of that imagery in external forms of procedure (Saturn).

Venus is the ruler of the formative and image-making power of subconsciousness. It is the dominant Key of the second row. Here her power is linked with that of the Moon, represented in Tarot by the High Priestess.

To square our lives with the order of the universe, we must invoke the power of intuition. We learn from observation what is below in the field of sensation. However, we cannot know the meaning of our observations unless it is imparted to us by the Hierophant.

When we are instructed, we become partakers in the Life-power perfect memory of the significance of existence. The One Spirit knows the nature of the glorious opportunity, which presents itself to us in the guise of a terrifying problem. It will share that knowledge with us if we listen. Therefore we attain the balance of personal mental powers represented by the third Key (6) of the second row.

The harmony between self-consciousness, subconsciousness, and the superconscious Self are the consequences of repeatedly listening to the Inner Voice and obeying its instruction. Then come discrimination and the ability to use the law represented by Key 8.

When we are obedient to the Inner Voice, the suggestions transmitted to the human level of subconsciousness are symbolized by the woman in Key 8. They are constructive, and they descend automatically to the subhuman levels typified by the lion. We do not have to trouble ourselves about this transmission. It works without conscious interference on our part. *All the powers of nature obey us without question when we obey the Inner Voice. This, in the plainest of language, is the Great Secret of practical occultism.*

$$7 - 9 - 10 - 4$$

The third row of Keys begins with the Chariot, related to Cancer (♋), and the combined influences of the Moon and Jupiter. Those who would meet and solve their problems must continually remind themselves that their existence is a vehicle of expression for the universal Life-power. Our lives are direct expressions of the cosmic order, and manifestations of power ever victorious. No matter what the appearance of the moment may be, each of us is in precisely the situation required for the expression of the Order and Beauty of the One Being. Over us, ever observing our progress, stands the Silent Watcher, lighting the upward path (Key 9).

The slightest detail of our daily lives can be excluded from the sequence of Divine Manifestation. Whatever seems to be otherwise is evidence of temporary delusion, and even that delusion has its place in the Great Plan (Key 10).

Not for one moment is the vigilance of the Supreme Self relaxed. Not for one moment is there any cessation of the supervision which the Life-power exercises over the process of its self-manifestation. That process includes the life history of every human being (Key 4).

12 – 2 – 1 – 15

The fourth row begins with the Hanged Man, a symbol of the dependence of personal existence upon the support of the Tree of Universal Life. The message of Key 12 is we must make conscious surrender of our existence to the supervision of the Life-power.

We must practice this because it does not "come naturally." All the superficial evidence of the senses is against it. To overcome the influence of this sensory illusion, together with the hypnosis of delusion, which affects the race mind with the feeling of separateness, continual repetition of the conscious attitude of surrender is required.

Then surrender becomes second nature. When this happens, we begin to read the scroll of the Universal Memory. The sense of personal separateness prevents us from doing so now. Our belief that we are separate is a suggestion accepted by the subconscious mind. The response keeps us from reading that part of the High Priestess' scroll, which was inscribed before our physical birth into this present incarnation. When we realize our personal life is continuous with the stream of universal existence, we begin to recover knowledge of events that occurred before the date of our birth (Key 2).

This knowledge is essential to solving the problems that confront us. The inverted pentagram on the Devil's head is a symbol that every problem is one of ignorance. The root of ignorance is some form of the delusion of separateness. This ignorance is to be overcome by conscious mental activity, represented Key 1.

The transforming power has its field of operation at the self-conscious level. We have to be consciously and intentionally receptive to the descent of knowledge and power from superconscious levels. Also, we must act deliberately as transmitters of that knowledge and power to the plane of subconsciousness.

Everything depends on our appraisal of the place of personality in the cosmic order. If we know who we are, understand our self-conscious mind, know its powers, and use them correctly, then everything else follows automatically (Key 1).

This may sound too easy, but the Masters declare with Jesus: "My yoke is easy, and my burden is light." (Matthew 11:30) Consider the final Key of the series. The fearsome aspect of the Devil is a delusion. There is no reality in the universe corresponding to this dreadful figure. The perfect knowledge of the Life-power has no problems or ignorance. Your true Self knows what you must do to be free from the bondage that seems to limit you. Mentally relate yourself to that liberating power, and you will find the solution to the problem (Key 15).

MEDITATIONS

1st DAY: Keys 0, 14, 13, 3. My true Self perceives the vision of my joyous destiny. That Self directs the alchemical operation, which transmutes my personality into an adequate vehicle of its manifestation. In the field of my personal life, it reaps the harvest of Yesterday and sows the seed of Tomorrow.

My earthly life today is the realization of the heavenly pattern.

2nd DAY: Keys 11, 5, 6, 8. Today I live the Law. I hear and obey the Inner Voice. Consciously and subconsciously, I am in harmony with my true Self.

All power is given me of my father in heaven.

3rd DAY: Keys 7, 9, 10, 4. My personal life is the field of cosmic manifestation. I move upward toward what I am. My inevitable destiny is release from every form of delusion.

My birthright is perfect mastery of circumstances.

4th DAY: Keys 12, 2, 1, 15. Today I renounce every appearance of separateness. This day's thoughts and deeds are related to all that has ever gone before. I know my rightful place in the Great Whole.

My problem is my opportunity.

5th DAY: Keys 15, 10, 5, 0. I fear no evil. For this day's experience is part of the manifestation of perfect order. Let me hear the Voice that expounds its true meaning.

Let me share now in the heavenly vision.

6th DAY: Keys 3, 6, 9, 12. The door of opportunity opens to me today. Let me have discrimination to perceive it. Let me always remember that I advance steadily toward the heights of conscious mastery.

My personal life is the earthly utterance of the heavenly word.

TAROT INTERPRETATION

Chapter 18

The 2nd Stage of Spiritual Unfoldment

The Tarot Magic Square for this lesson is

4	14	15	1
9	7	6	12
5	11	10	8
16	2	3	13

$4 + 14 + 15 + 1 = 34$
$9 + 7 + 6 + 12 = 34$
$5 + 11 + 10 + 8 = 34$
$16 + 2 + 3 + 13 = 34$

The sum of the numbers from 1 to 16 is 136.

For these lessons, we use the four horizontal rows of these magic squares, reading them from right to left. In formulating the meditations, the same reading is followed for the first four days. The meditation for the fifth day follows the diagonal upward from left lower to right upper corner, and the meditation for the sixth day follows the descending diagonal from top-left to lower-right corner. This is not the only way to read the square. Every row is read in either direction and as their addition is always the same, so is the meaning. The meaning emerges from a different sequence of ideas, according to the course of the movement along the line. The sequences not utilized in these lessons should be studied, along with the ones given in this instruction.

For example, the outcome of the sequence 4, 14, 15, 1 is the same as 1, 15, 14, 4. The number 34 represents the outcome, which is the sum of any row in this magic square. For example, the meaning of this square (34) is seven (4 + 3 = 7), considered as the expression of 4 through the agency of 3. The number 7 is the Chariot representing the power of the Emperor (4), working through the agency of the Empress (3).

There are many ways by which this result may be reached. There are four horizontal, four vertical, and two diagonal rows, all adding to 34, or ten in all. Since each of these may be read in two directions, the square shows twenty combinations of arriving at the same result. Consider each combination because no two ways are alike since the progress of ideas follows a different order.

The 2nd Stage of Spiritual Unfoldment – Awakening

This week begins with the Magician and ends with the Tower. The whole square is concerned with the second stage of spiritual unfoldment, symbolized by Key 16. Like 34, notice that 16 also reduces to seven (1 + 6 = 7). Therefore 34 and 16 are related to each other.

There can be no awakening for an inattentive human. Those who are content with superficialities never reach the second stage of unfoldment. This does not mean that some are doomed to eternal bondage. All awakening is the consequence of aroused attention. Nobody remains forever content with superficialities. But some awaken gently, while others are rudely stimulated by painful experiences, which force them to consider the nature of their surroundings attentively. Perhaps our earlier awakenings are of the sort pictured by Key 16. The time comes when our houses of delusion are overthrown without the accompaniments of terror suggested by the symbolism of Key 16. In a measure, we are prepared for the event. Experience has taught us that no problem is solved until some structure of ignorance is knocked down. Even then, often, we are astounded when the event comes to pass. For years, we cherished some delusion. Then, all at once, we have a glimpse of reality, and over goes one more stronghold of error. Something we always supposed to be true turns out to be just the opposite.

1 – 15 – 14 – 4

Our power comes from above, as do higher forms of knowledge. However, at the self-conscious level that transformations occur. Everything constituting our environment is subject to our self-conscious thought and is a reflection of thought. Self-consciousness *is* the Magician, *is* the Transformer. We do not have to make it so, nor is occult training directed to this end. On the contrary, esoteric practice is concerned only with the right application of our inherent magical power (Key 1).

Whenever we are confronted by any appearance of restriction and bondage, understand an appearance is a form conjured up by our magic power. Difficult as it is to accept, the occult doctrine is unequivocal.

EVERY APPEARANCE OF ADVERSITY IS BUILT UP BY THE MENTAL POWER WORKING THROUGH THE PERSON TO WHOM THAT APPEARANCE IS PRESENTED (Key 15).

Therefore the alchemist-magician looks upon no situation as being adverse. We adopt the "confident attitude" of Rudolf Steiner. We have no fear of circumstance because we enjoy communion with the Lord of Circumstance. Anything that appears to be evil we regard with particular interest. Like the shepherd in the New Testament parable, he is interested in these lost sheep of the House of Israel. To set in order what seems to be a disorder is to treat evil as raw material for transmutation into the very forms of expression which will best suit our purpose. This is the secret of our work (Key 14).

Occult practice does not *confer* magic power, nor enable one to *attain* it. What it does is to make us aware, through experience and reason, that we *have* magical power. The training is the orderly exercise of our inherent power. The goal of this practice is to see objectively our circumstances agree with our mentally conceived patterns (Key 4).

12 − 6 − 7 − 9

A theurgist, or "God-worker," has no power to impose on the world around them a pattern that represents their idea of the way they want things to appear. A theurgist formulates patterns following the way things are. They know they live in a Universe on which we depend for every good and perfect gift. A theurgist recognizes the absolute dependability of the laws and forces of the universe (Key 12). Their practice leads to perfect reciprocal activity between the self-conscious and subconscious minds, and the harmonious relation of both to the super-conscious Self (Key 6). Therefore a theurgist is a conscious vehicle of the Life-power, and their magic succeeds because their "personal" volition is the expression of the cosmic order (Key 7). "My will is to do the will of him that sent me," is an accurate expression of the theurgist state of mind (Key 9).

8 – 10 – 11 – 5

The theurgist tames wild beasts because they know the forces in their environment are essentially friendly. Nature is never an enemy, but an ally (Key 8). The play of forces around a theurgist is seen as the manifestation of the laws at work in their being. A theurgist recognizes the highest and dominant power in the cosmic mechanism is identical with the Principle of Individuality at the heart of their life (Key 10). A theurgist understands they are incarnate Law and restores the Law-giver to His rightful place on the throne in the palace of personality (Key 11). This understanding is not a consequence of sterile speculation or reasoning, but the result of a vivid interior perception, which has been described as hearing the Inner Voice (Key 5).

In every ritual of initiation, the candidate passes through a mystical death. This dissolution refers to the passing away of the old concept of separate personality. The separate mortal human must die, to reborn as an immortal, one with the Father, before we exercise our magical powers (Key 13). New mental imagery takes the place of the old race-thought. The idea by the word "human" must be reconceived.

From Revelation: 2: 17: "Whoever has ears, let them hear what the Spirit says to the churches. To the one who is victorious, I will give some of the hidden manna. I will also give that person a white stone with a new name written on it, known only to the one who receives it."

In occult schools, the initiate adopts a new name representing their highest aspiration. This is a mental concept of themselves that their work is intended to build into their personality (Key 3). This new name is not new. Instead, it is a reconstitution or restoration of something which was forgotten. The Chaldean Oracle says: "Explore the river of the soul, whence, or in what order, you have come; so that although you have become a servant to the body, you may rise again to the Order from which you descended, joining works to sacred reason."

And the parable of the Prodigal Son, where he "came to himself." The basis of all magical work is a recollection of the actual meaning and power of the Self (Key 2). The lightning-flash of inspiration, which awakens us, and at the same time overthrows our prisons of delusion, is a flash of self-recollection. When we remember what we are, we escape from the bondage of the sense of separateness (Key 16).

16 – 11 – 6 – 1

Nearly always, our errors have their roots in fear, and generally, these fears are part of the race inheritance. The occult point-of-view is the reverse of common sense. The fourfold occult maxim says.

TO KNOW, TO WILL, TO DARE, TO BE SILENT. The race mind has little courage. Popular proverbs disguise cowardice as prudence, and we are all more or less infected by this poison (Key 16). Absolute faith is indispensable to the practical occultist. Confidence established by careful weighing of evidence, faith arrived at by careful discrimination (Key 11). Such faith is found when persistent effort has made subconsciousness a clear mirror, reflecting super-conscious knowledge into the field of self-consciousness (Key 6). The beginning of discrimination is the mental attitude of the Magician— continual endeavor to keep in touch with the power source above the conscious level, combined with habitual alertness, directed steadily to watchful consideration of every detail of self-conscious experience (Key 1).

4 – 7 – 10 – 13

It cannot be said too often that magic effects no change in the essential nature of things. Neither does it modify the orderly sequence of cosmic manifestation. The magician awakens from a dream of delusion; that is all. They change their point-of-view. They stop thinking of the world as their adversary or something opposed to their will. Instead, they see it as their domain, as the instrument of self-expression, as something subordinate to the Spirit within them, which is their true Self. By seeing it, they experience it (Key 4). For such a person, the need for artificial means of self-protection ceases. All the counsels of cowardice which the world calls "prudence" have no meaning. They rest securely in the understanding their personality is a vehicle for the power of the ever-victorious Lord of Creation (Key 7).

They have transferred their consciousness from the outer rim of the Wheel of Fortune, with its succession of ups and downs, to the spiritual center where there are no fluctuations (Key 10). Death doesn't frighten them, because they made contact with that which is unaffected by external change. In contact, they find that death is an aspect of the activity of the One Self. For the skeleton reaper of Key 13 is a representation of the transforming power of that Self, even as the other Keys of the series are representations of other aspects of the same power (Key 13).

Summary

These are some of the meanings of this tableau, but they do not exhaust the significance of the Keys. You will do well to make entries in your notebook concerning any point which occurs to you as you look at the Keys.

At the beginning of each practice period, laid out the entire magic square and dedicate at least five minutes to inspecting the Keys. Observe their relations with one another. During the last five minutes, use only the four Keys with the day's meditation.

Another hint. In every row of Keys, notice what Key links another to the one which follows it. For example, in the top row, the first card is Key 1, and the second is Key 15. The link between these two is Key 14. The link between Keys 14 and 4 is Key 10. Follow out this hint with the other rows.

MEDITATIONS

1st DAY: Keys 1, 15, 14, 4. I am a direct agent of Limitless Life. The world I see is the projection of my mental patterns. My true Self transmutes every semblance of adversity into a means for the perfect manifestation of my heart's desire.

I rule my domain.

2nd DAY: Keys 12, 6, 7, 9. Because I am fundamentally one with the Source of all existence, all things work together for my good. The elements of my consciousness are in harmony with themselves and with the super-conscious Life, which is their Source. My volition is not of myself but is a calm expression of the universal order.

The light that lights every human shines on my path today.

3rd DAY: Keys 8, 10, 11, 5. All Nature and her forces are my allies. The motive power of the cosmic mechanism is seated in my heart. I am the incarnate Law.

The word of power utters itself within the sanctuary of my inner life.

4th DAY: Keys 13, 3, 2, 16. Today I die to all the delusions of the past. The New Image comes to life in my heart of hearts. I recollect my place in the universal order.

I awaken from delusion.

5th DAY: Keys 16, 11, 6, 1. I dare to be what I truly am. My faith is immovable, for I know what must appear as the inevitable consequence of what I have already discovered.

It is my prerogative to be an administrator of the cosmic will.

6th DAY: Keys 4, 7, 10, 13. The Spirit of Life, which I am, rules all things. It is ever victorious. It is even now the master of every condition.

This day i dissolve all illusion.

TAROT INTERPRETATION

Chapter 19

The 3rd Stage of Spiritual Unfoldment – Revelation

The Tarot Magic Square for this lesson is:

5	15	16	2
10	8	7	13
6	12	11	9
17	3	4	14

$5 + 15 + 16 + 2 = 38.$
$10 + 8 + 7 + 13 = 38.$
$6 + 12 + 11 + 9 = 38.$
$17 + 3 + 4 + 14 = 38.$

The sum of the numbers from 2 to 17 is 152.

Its constant summation is 38. The meaning of the twenty possible combinations is represented by Key 11, Justice. It is the working of the power represented by Key 8 through the agency symbolized by Key 3. This square also corresponds to the third stage of spiritual unfoldment, as represented by Key 17 – Revelation.

This square represents the manifestation of the Faithful Intelligence, Lamed (ל), and Key 11. This square is aspects of the Faithful Intelligence, which are the outcome of the Intelligence of the Secret of Works (Key 8) through the agency of the Luminous Intelligence (Key 3). The whole tableau relates to the unveiling of truth in the practice of meditation (Key 17).

The summation of every row of Keys is 38 and may be represented by placing Keys 3 and 8 side by side. From the previous chapter, we learned that Key 5 is taken into consideration in studying this tableau because Key 5 is the link between Keys 3 and 8.

Meditation unveils the truth and establishes faith. Meditation is a practice that utilizes the law that all subhuman forms of universal energy are under the control of human subconsciousness. This law, consciously recognized and used to develop creative imagination, is what enables us to establish the true magical faith. A faith that moves mountains overcomes disease, banishes poverty, and makes for happiness. Not blind faith, the woman seated on the throne of Justice, wears no blindfold. The faith of the practicing magician is based on tried and tested knowledge. Their faith is an imaginative extension into the future of that which they know now. *The magical faith is a confident expectation that what is will continue to be.* This is the opposite of the blind faith, which petitions to a God who is thought to be susceptible to flattery. To ask God to ward off calamity, to plead with Him for special favors, is invariably to pray amiss. For such prayer assumes that God is capricious and the author of calamity.

Occult doctrine agrees with Isaiah in declaring that the One Life-power is the source of all conditions, including those called evil.

> I form light and create darkness. I make peace and create calamity. I am Yahweh, who does all these things. – Isaiah 45:7.

The prayer of faith is answered, even though the God to whom it is addressed be wrongly conceived. Consider the life of George Mueller, who conducted several orphanages in England on the assumption that God answers prayer. An occult student would find it difficult to believe in the actual existence of a God, such as the one to whom George Mueller addressed his prayers.

What is the explanation? Simply that blind faith has in it an element of truth. God is an unfailing source of supply for any good work. Mueller's faith was better than his theology. Also, his faith never wavered, no matter what the appearances might be. He never prayed that calamity might be averted. On the contrary, all his prayers were affirmative. He never lost his vision of the Life-power as a treasury of inexhaustible abundance.

True magical faith has the same steadfast quality because a practical occultist accumulates evidence that the Life-power is dependable. Therefore we never doubt that the mental patterns we conceive are realized as objective conditions manifest on the physical plane.

2 – 16 – 15 – 5

The beginning of his faith is in recollection. By careful examination of the memory record of our experience, we learn to discern the operation of law in the events of our life. The study of our past is a regular part of our meditation practice. Every day, we review the events of that day that we may see how the law has been manifest in those events. We also devote time to examine the circumstances of our earlier years, carrying ourselves back to his earliest memories (Key 2). As a result of this practice, we overcome many of his earliest delusions. We have the perspective of wider experience and a higher type of knowledge. Thus we see how erroneous were many of the suppositions we once mistook for truth (Key 16). We recall instances of seeming adversity and see that often, the obstacles and limitations which distressed us were the cause of our advancement (Key 15).

In addition to the practice of recollection, we practice listening to the Inner Voice. Then we begin to understand how we have been under guidance, even in those periods of his life, when he seemed to be walking in complete darkness (Key 5).

13 – 7 – 8 – 10

To understand the working of the law of transformation, we learn the futility of the ignorant desire to keep conditions the same. We see how the law of eternal progress demands that old forms must give place to new. Therefore, we eventually discover the mystery of life behind the veil of death. One result of meditation is the recovery of memories of past incarnations. Once the student has seen that our present life is one of a series, all fear of death leaves them (Key 13). From that time forward, we understand that the ephemeral personality is a vehicle for the eternal Self (Key 7). As we practice recollection and meditation, it becomes evident that the external conditions of our personal experience have always been the objectification of our mental attitudes (Key 8).

Furthermore, we discover that the mental attitudes that are pain-bearing were beneficent, in that they brought corrective experience. Then we see that our mental unfoldment is a cosmic as well as a personal process. We trace our progress upward from earlier states of comparative ignorance to his present stage of better understanding and perceive that every step was inevitable. From then on, we do not doubt the perfect completion of the process (Key 10).

9 – 11 – 12 – 6

In the earlier stages of spiritual development, there is a strong sense of effort, even a struggle. In the early stages, the delusion of separateness is strong within us. But all sages testify that this sense of effort is a delusion. We do not work. The power of the One Self carries us upward, and we are always under its beneficent supervision (Key 9). The practical occultist learns this truth by examining the record of their own past life, and by careful observation of the lives of their contemporaries. Thus we discover that every human personality is a direct expression of the law which maintains the perfect equilibrium of the cosmic order (Key 11).

A direct consequence of this knowledge is the mental attitude of complete resignation. The true Initiate knows that the law is at work because they see it in various phases of their life and has observed it in the lives of others. Thus they surrender to it without any reservation whatever (Key 12).

This does not come all at once. There must be steady practice. The records of memory must be scanned with great care. They must be stripped of all disguise. The outcome of occult practice, which is similar to psychoanalysis, is to establish a harmonious reciprocal relation between the self-conscious and subconscious of our mental life. The perfected condition thus attained is represented in the symbolism of Key 6.

Right meditation leads to the Knowledge and Conversation of the Holy Guardian Angel. In meditation, one perceives that their life is and has always been, an alchemical operation directed by that Angel. We do not make progress. Our improved state of consciousness, with its accompanying increase in control of our environment, is the outcome of the operation of the Self upon its vehicle, our personality.

Consider the words of Jesus, "If I am lifted up, will draw all men unto me." These words imply the presence of a power superior to the personal man Jesus. That power, which Jesus called "Father," is the Divine Operator who tempers our chemistry so that we become more suitable vehicles for expressing the One Life (Key 14).

No part of our equipment is separate from the universal Being. When we see things as they are, we share the Divine Vision. Our command of circumstance is one with the Universal Dominion, expressing in the conditions of time and space that constitute our environment (Key 4). The subconscious gestation of mental images is a consequence of new ideas within our field of awareness. It is a universal process. There is no plane of being where the universal Life-power is not present. There is no phase of activity in which it is not the real Actor (Key 3).

Truth is identical to the One Spirit. Though it may seem that we uncover the truth by meditation, the time will come when we understand that we are disposed of by the One Self to adopt the practice of meditation. Meditation is an example of the method whereby the real nature of the One Life unveils itself to human consciousness. God, in us, reveals Himself to Himself (Key 17).

17 – 12 – 7 – 2

Patanjali says meditation is an unbroken flow of knowledge in a particular object. Reflection makes evident that meditation is participation in the One Spirit's continuous flow of knowledge in all things. To meditate is to be identified with the Divine Consciousness of some aspect of reality. This is why occult literature emphasizes the importance of meditation (Key 17). In meditation, the personal mentation, intermittent and spasmodic, is suspended. Thus a sage in Samadhi is in a state of trance and the deepest stages the trance counterfeits death (Key 12).

This suspension of personal activity is accompanied by an enhancement of real consciousness. The personal vehicle is at rest. The senses are quiescent. The Self is wide awake, and there is no cessation of Self-consciousness. They who emerge from the trance of meditation does not ask, "Where am I?" Neither do they make inquiries as to what they have said or done, for they have never lost consciousness.

Instead, consciousness was functioning at a higher level. From that level, they invariably bring back knowledge and the ability to exercise power beyond the limits of ordinary personal consciousness (Key 7). In Samadhi, we remember what we are, and the glory and power of that recollection manifest themselves (Key 2).

$$5 - 8 - 11 - 14$$

Meditation begins with a careful examination of the record of your existence. This is combined with the attitude of listening for the Inner Voice because it explains the significance of that record. This must be a daily practice (Key 5). The result is the knowledge of the Great Secret. This knowledge can never be imparted by human words. Only its bare outline is given in any occult writing. It is symbolized in the Tarot by Key 8. From the inner revelation of this Great Secret, the practical occultist derives their open-eyed, magical faith (Key 11). The immediate outcome of that faith is the Knowledge and Conversation of the Holy Guardian Angel. To know that Guiding Presence, to share in its perception to receive through it the wisdom and power of the Pure Spirit— this is the consequence of meditation (Key 14).

MEDITATIONS

1st DAY: Keys 2, 16, 15, 5. I remember today what I am. This recollection enables me to destroy erroneous mental constructions. I face my problems gladly, for they are my opportunities to demonstrate power.

My life this day is a lesson in the mysteries of the higher law.

2nd DAY: Keys 13, 7, 8, 10. All transformations of circumstance are for my good. My body and my environment are plastic vehicles for the limitless power and wisdom of the Eternal Spirit. They are the out-picturing of my vision of the Self.

The life of this day is a cycle of the eternal existence.

3rd DAY: Keys 9, 11, 12, 6. It is not I who do this day's work, not I who enjoy this day's pleasures, not I who experience these days' difficulties. All these events are part of the balancing of Heaven's accounts. I am but the witness of the operation.

Let me quietly observe the perfect work.

4th DAY: Keys 14, 4, 3, 17. I submit joyfully to the tests this day brings. Through me, the Universal Dominion expresses its perfect command of circumstance. It works below the surface of my consciousness to develop more beautiful forms of expression.

God in me unveils himself to himself.

5th DAY: Keys 17, 12, 7, 2. Truth is the basis of my existence. Nothing can separate me from its unfailing support. No slightest detail of my life is a manifestation of Universal Spirit.

I remember my creator.

6th DAY: Keys 5, 8, 11, 14. Be Thou my Guide, O Teacher of all teachers. Let me be strong in Thy strength. Let me be faithful in thought, word, and deed.

I am overshadowed by the protecting presence of the almighty.

TAROT INTERPRETATION

Chapter 20

The 4th Stage of Spiritual Unfoldment – Organization[1]

The Tarot Magic Square for this lesson is,

6	16	17	3
11	9	8	14
7	13	12	10
18	4	5	15

$6 + 16 + 17 + 3 = 42.$
$11 + 9 + 8 + 14 = 42.$
$7 + 13 + 12 + 10 = 42.$
$18 + 4 + 5 + 15 = 42.$

The sum of the numbers from 3 to 18 is 168.

The constant summation is 42, shows of Key 6, The Lovers, as the manifestation of memory working through Key 4 (observation). This square also corresponds to the fourth stage of spiritual unfoldment, represented by Key 18 – Organization.

Key 6 represents the Disposing Intelligence corresponding to Zain (ז). Key 2 stands for the Uniting Intelligence and Gimel (ג). Key 4 is the Constituting Intelligence corresponding to Heh (ה). The *Book of Formation* says the Uniting Intelligence is the "essence of glory." This essence is mind-stuff, symbolized by the robe of the High Priestess, blue and shimmering because it represents the element Water, the Astral Fluid, which solidifies into the forms on the physical plane. The Astral Fluid is utilized through the activity of the Constituting Intelligence, which "constitute creative force in pure darkness." The Constituting Intelligence operates principally through sight. This phase of the Life-power's activity leads to the correct vision.

The power of vision is a spiritual power, whereby the Astral Fluid is condensed into visible, external forms. The sight center in the brain exercises its highest functions when metaphysical light streams through and energizing the pineal body. *The pineal gland is like a lens through which Astral Light, in fluidic form, is projected into the external conditions of the physical plane.* Read attentively, for this is the essential secret of magic or theurgy. They who see genuinely is an immediate instrument of the Constituting Intelligence, which builds the forms and conditions of the external world. The mysterious power of transformation exerted by adepts, the ability to perform miracles, to heal sick bodies, to bring about changes in the constitution of physical forms, is the Constituting Intelligence.

To see genuinely is to be able to control the positive and negative currents of the Astral Light. These are the solar and lunar currents of Prana. In *Nature's Finer Forces,* "To those men who practice, and thus always keep the sun and moon in proper order, knowledge of the past and future becomes as easy as if they were in their hand." In the alchemical books, the Great Work is said to consist in control of the Sun and Moon. Note the implication here. The Sun and Moon are the luminaries of day and night, the sources of light whereby we are enabled to see. Their light is the basis of our power of vision. Therefore to control the solar and lunar currents is to control our sight power. Hence the alchemical books tell us the Great Work is performed by the Sun and Moon, with the aid of Mercury.

You will remember that the Disposing Intelligence attributed to Zain (ז) is also related to the Mercurial sign Gemini (♊), represented by Key 6 in Tarot.

Mercury is the Magician. The Emperor is the same as the Magician after his union with the High Priestess has transformed her into the Empress, who bears his children. Therefore Mercury is connected with the letter Heh (ה), although Heh in the *Sepher Yetzirah* corresponds to Aries, ruled by Mars.

188

The head and brain, and particularly the eyes and the sight center, are the instruments of what is personified as Mercury. The force at work through these centers is the Mars energy. In Key 1, the Magician wears a red outer garment – the color of Mars. In the Tarot color scale, Gemini is orange. On the Tree of Life, orange is given to Splendor, the eighth Sephirah – the Sphere of Mercury. Orange is a mixture of red (Mars) and yellow (Mercury). All this is involved and technical, but it is included for the benefit of students who have an aptitude for following up clues leading to the solution of alchemical and magical problems. Readers with different skills need only remember that these correspondences are that the mental part of the real vision is Mercurial, while the force involved is represented by Mars.

3 – 17 – 16 – 6

Seeing is an act of imagination and a manifestation of the laws of optics. Our physical vision has to be supplemented by mental imagery (Key 3). The perception of real relationships is super-sensual, the consequence of meditation.

To see requires the correlation of all our senses and the sublimation of their reports into a higher order of knowing (Key 17). From superficial sense knowledge, we gain material for the structure of error, sooner or later, to be overthrown by a sudden influx of light from superconsciousness (Key 16). The balance of conscious and subconscious activities symbolized by the Lovers cannot be maintained while the sense of separateness persists. When imprisoned in delusion, the conscious and unconscious phases of our mentality are in disguise. Thus the falling figures in Key 16 are shown clothed, but in Key 6, the man and the woman are nude to show that neither hides anything from the other.

14 – 8 – 9 – 11

Before the Great Work is finished, it seems we are doing experiments. When the operation reaches its term, we know our personality has been the subject of the transmutation performed by the true Self, from superconscious levels (Key 14). The conscious mind is only a transmitter of light from above. In the Tarot tableau given in *Tarot Fundamentals*, the Magician is placed over Strength. This shows that the subconscious modifications come from him. At the same time, he is shown lifting his right hand that holds the wand. His left-hand points downward to indicate that he is a transmitter of energy drawn from above, which he directs to planes below.

The power which tames the lion in Key 8, has its origin in the superconscious. It comes from the height where the Hermit stands, and its effect is concerned with processes of body-building related to Virgo (♍). The progress of a human being along the Path of Return, which leads to adeptship and from adeptship to mastery, is a series of bodily transformations. It is a chemical process of purification and sublimation, which results in the weaving of a finer and subtler vehicle for the Spirit (Key 9). It is also a process which brings about the elimination of the grosser elements of the physical organism, and the fine adjustment of all the forces within it (Key 11).

10 – 12 – 13 – 7

Our unfoldment is more than personal. It is a unique manifestation of universal laws and forces in the field of action represented by the life of a particular personality. The whole universe manifests within and through each of us (Key 10). Our lives are always dependent on the cosmic life, but until we reach a particular stage of unfoldment, we do not know this. We come to this stage, we are aware of our dependence and gladly submit ourselves to the cosmic life (Key 12). This results in the dissolution of seemingly separated personalities, and this dissolution is the "mystic death" (Key 13). It is a transfer of consciousness from the vehicle to THAT which is the rider in the vehicle. It is a change from the bustle and disquiet of separateness to the still calm of the One Life. Therefore is the chariot, in Key 7, shown at rest, with the two sphinxes couchant.

15 – 5 – 4 – 18

In reality, there is no adversary. As humans progress in understanding, they synthesize the hosts of devils imagined by his ancestors into one Prince of Darkness. Even this Enemy is a figment of our imagination. A page of cipher manuscripts contains the clues enabling a cryptographer to decipher it. So do the appearance of antagonism that the universe presents to the uninitiated reveal to the instructed that all things are working for the liberation of human's spiritual powers (Key 15).

Sooner or later, every human reaches the stage of unfoldment, where the meaning of life is made known, the significance is revealed, and the Way of Liberation is made plain. The Inner Voice speaks, and as we listen and obey, delusion vanishes (Key 15).

Then we see things as they really are. This vision is a perception of an order which is eternally present. The vision does not impose order in place of disorder, although that is what seems to happen. People with astigmatism see outlines of objects that are blurred. However, universal processes are never disorderly, nor antagonistic to human welfare. When our vision is corrected, we see the order which has been there all the while (Key 4).

This better seeing is the result of a bodily transformation. It is brought about by the sublimation of the natural body — by a gradual alteration in the body chemistry and structure. This makes the physical organism a suitable vehicle for the manifestation of rates of vibratory activity higher than those expressed through the physical body of the natural man (Key 18).

The fact that adeptship and mastery are consequences of profound alterations in physical chemistry and structure cannot be overemphasized. In these days, there is a tendency to accept the error that liberation is a matter of mind alone— or something to do with higher planes, to the exclusion of the physical (Key 18). The mystic death is a real dissolution of physical cells— an elimination of cells impregnated by the consciousness of separateness (Key 13). The removal is automatic. It is imperceptible, yet it is actual. When the animal nature is brought under control, it ceases to be the animal nature (Key 8). The initial impulses which effect this transformation are passed down into the cellular level from the subconsciousness, and they follow changes in our mental imagery, modifications made by acts of concentration (Key 3).

6 – 9 – 12 – 15

Continual practice in discrimination, frequent exercise of intellectual power, to the end that the functions of conscious and subconscious are rightly exercised is required to effect these changes. This may seem to contradict what has just been said, to the effect that the work is performed by the Higher Self. The contradiction is superficial. In Key 6, it is the power of the angel above the man and woman which is specialized in their particular activities. The angel is the real Actor.

Nevertheless, what is below the angle also acts. To say the One Self does the work does not absolve us from the duty of effort. **So long as effort seems necessary, it is required**. We are not working against the illusion of separateness. It is the delusion that fails to recognize the illusion and fails to understand how that illusion is necessary to the Life-power's self-expression in the universe and the life of humans (Key 6).

The real Self of every human being is the Eternal Watcher, pictured in Tarot as the Hermit. As long as one is not entirely identified with that One, the illusion of separateness persists. It requires us to act as if our practice and efforts bring about the changes through which we attain to liberation (Key 9).

Whether we know it or not, we are dependent on the universal Life-power. Whether we realize it or not, we do nothing of ourselves. Knowing this marks a stage of spiritual unfoldment. We ripen into it, as a fruit which is acid and poisonous in its green state ripens into sweetness and healthfulness in due season (Key 12).

With such knowledge comes a new attitude toward seeming adversity, the criticism of others, and the mental state of those who misjudge and make false and defamatory claims against us. The unripe person hates their adversaries, longs for a day when he shall be freed from enemies, damns those who speak ill of them, and questions the justice of cosmic law. They who are ripe love their enemies, knows the accuracy of the proverb, "sweet are the uses of adversity." They are compassionate towards the mental darkness of those who misunderstand and condemn them. They look upon discomfort as a signal that they have an adjustment to make, somewhere in their mechanism (Key 15).

Summary

Persons attracted to Tarot and similar studies are approaching ripeness. They had glimpses of a higher state of human existence. Thus they have attracted the notice of those riper humans who are ahead of us on the Path of Return. From those riper elder brothers and sisters of humanity comes all teaching like this. It is based on their own experience, an experience we may share if we choose.

MEDITATIONS

1st DAY: Keys 3, 17, 16, 6. The harvest of wisdom ripens in the field of my subconsciousness. Day by day, my vision of truth becomes more manifest. I welcome the overthrow of my former errors.

The overshadowing presence disposes me to faithfulness.

2nd DAY: Keys 14, 8, 9, 11. In this day's experiences, the One Life refines and purifies my personality. I am made whole by Universal Medicine. The One Will forms my flesh and blood, according to its perfect pattern.

The law of liberty sets me free.

3rd DAY: Keys 10, 12, 13, 7. The Life-power already is all that I want it to be. Its power is the immovable basis of all my achievements. That power dissolves everything in my personality that seems to obstruct its free self-expression.

I am being fashioned into a perfect vehicle for the victorious one.

4th DAY: Keys 15, 5, 4, 18. I fear no evil as I listen and obey the instruction of the Inner Voice, delusion vanishes. I see the heavenly order wherever I look.

I am being transformed into the likeness of the oneself, that self which sees naught but the perfection of its divine manifestation.

5th DAY: Keys 18, 13, 8, 3. Today marks another stage of progress along the Path of Return. Today marks the dissolution of some errors of the past. Today is a perfect expression of the inexhaustible strength of the One Life.

Today brings me nearer the goal of true wisdom.

6th DAY: Keys 6, 9, 12, 15. This day I manifest harmony; I look upward toward the heights. I rest secure in the knowledge of my union with the Life-power.

I renew my strength.

[1] Case explicitly states in the three previous chapters the stages of spiritual unfoldment. However, he says nothing about the last four stages in the last four lessons. It's implied. Also, the last question of the Tarot Interpretation test is naming the seven stages of spiritual unfoldment.

Chapter 21

The 5th Stage of Spiritual Unfoldment – Regeneration

The Tarot Magic Square for this lesson is

7	17	18	4
12	10	9	15
8	14	13	11
19	5	6	16

$7 + 17 + 18 + 4 = 46.$
$12 + 10 + 9 + 15 = 46.$
$8 + 14 + 13 + 11 = 46.$
$19 + 5 + 6 + 16 = 46.$

The sum of the numbers from 4 to 19 is 184.

The constant summation is 46. This indicates Key 10, The Wheel of Fortune, considered as the operation of the principle symbolized by Key 6, The Lovers, working through what is represented by Key 4, the Emperor.

Intelligence of Desirous Quest

Through its connection with the letter Kaph (כ), Key 10 is related to the 21st Path on the Tree of Life, named "The Seeking Intelligence." The *Sepher Yetzirah* says, "It is so-called because it receives the divine influx to bless all, everyone." *receives The Divine Influence which it distributes as a blessing to all modes of being*

The letter name Kaph (כף) means, the palm of a hand. *"a grasping hand"* And open palm is ready to receive. Comprehension is the fundamental meaning. What is comprehended is something *already* given. We become receptive to the universe before we grasp its significance. Therefore, a Qabalists is a receptive person. Your mental training rests the foundation of receptivity to the influx of the impulses of the Life-power.

These impulses come to us through the sense channels, from without, and from superconscious levels, through the inner senses. Right comprehension is the result of balancing the two kinds of impulse. From without, we receive impressions that make us aware of existence. From within, we receive the intuitions which enable us to grasp the meaning of the facts.

$$4 - 18 - 17 - 7$$

The Universal Mind, which eternally understands existence and its significance, is the immediate presence in every human personality (Key 4). The degree in which that presence is felt and expressed in personal consciousness is conditioned by the state of the individual organism. A developed body is more responsive and expresses of the heavenly vision – like a fine radio has greater range, selectivity, and sound quality than a cheap one (Key 18).

Right meditation is the method used to refine the physical vehicle. Contrary to outward appearances, a human in meditation is not passive. By an intense act of will, they maintain an unbroken flow of knowledge in some particular object. Meditation begins with intense concentration on a fact of sense-experience. The appearance of a passive body deep in the meditative trance is in sharp contrast to the intense activity within, characterizing true meditation (Key 17). The outer vehicle is quiet, but the inner life is active and alert (Key 7).

After preliminary training in concentration, meditation should be used in connection with a particular object suggested by the problem uppermost in the student's life. The appearances of diversity which constitute a problem are caused by our ignorance of some element of the situation. The practical occultist faces their challenge squarely. They do not attempt to avoid it. They know from experience that every problem contains its answer, and in meditation, looks for the answer (Key 15). They know that the real Self, above and behind his personality, already knows the answer, and in their meditation seeks to make themselves receptive to the influx of higher knowledge (Key 9).

The underlying principle is that no circumstance is separate from the unbroken succession of events constituting the universal order. The conditions which seem to be adverse are aspects of the universal law, whose relation to the whole and ourselves we fail to perceive. Meditation enables us to receive from super-conscious levels the Life-power's perfect knowledge of the significance of any given situation (Key 10).

One of the means to attain comprehension is the mental attitude of receptivity to the supporting presence of the Life-power. We recognize that our life-expression is a manifestation, in time and space, of the universal Life. We surrender to that Life, and the more complete our surrender, the more our personality expresses the Life-power's command over circumstances. We submit our existence to the direction of the Life-power (Key 12).

The proverbial wisdom of the race is against it. Nothing in ordinary experience seems to support the occult doctrine. As one approaches what the esoteric schools call ripeness, a dim realization that one's existence is a manifestation of universal activities dawn in the mind of the seeker (Key 11).

There is a steady, almost imperceptible growth in consciousness. The student passes from vague awareness to the "mystic death" that dissolves their former personality and transforms the motivation of their existence (Key 13). After this transformation, the person knows that their being is a demonstration of the powers of the universal Life (Key 14).

The outcome of this demonstration is verification that the Higher Self is a master of all conditions. The first stages of the demonstration bring the student's body and all its forces under control of their mind. Later stages of growth bring animal life under their mental control. At more advanced stages of development make them master of the forces of the vegetable kingdom. The final stages of the Great Work give them command of the elemental forces of the inorganic or mineral kingdom. Those whom the Great Work reaches its final term appears to their contemporaries to be a worker of miracles. However, they understand they are an instrument of a higher power. Thus, Jesus says: "I cannot do anything of myself; as I hear, I judge, and my judgment is righteous, because I do not seek my will, but the will of him that has sent me." – John 5:30.

The adept understands that their command of circumstance is inherent in the Life-power. This command is an eternal fact. It was a reality long before it is demonstrated by the personality of adept. (Key 8).

16 – 6 – 5 – 19

Worldly wisdom regards a human's life as a personal affair. It is a fallacy that a human being is a separate unit. This false interpretation of personality must be destroyed before the Great Work is complete in the field of time and space – which is the setting for life (Key 16).

Careful examination of one's states of consciousness helps overcome the error. When the operations of the self-conscious and subconscious levels are watched closely, it becomes evident that the forces working do not originate in either of these two fields of action. Self-consciousness and subconsciousness are relative in their operation. We respond consciously and subconsciously to various stimuli, but the stimuli themselves originate outside the limits of personality. Even the power to respond comes from outside the personal field.

Anyone may discover this from observing the physical and mental activities of their existence. The angel in Key 6 represents the source of the powers expressed through personality. The symbolism of Key 6 shows the relation of the conscious and subconscious aspects of personality to the superconscious Life-power.

They who assume the presence of superconsciousness in their life are ready to be guided. Those who listen for its instruction and obey it will receive abundant evidence that their assumption is correct. Those who hear and follows the Inner Voice, it gives its wise counsel (Key 5).

Under its guidance, in due season, there is a regeneration of the personal life. This is the new birth, often mentioned in sacred and occult writings. It fashions the whole personality after a new image. The new person is imbued with the feeling that has experienced the mystery of resurrection (Key 19).

19 – 14 – 9 – 4

The "twice-born" or regenerated person turns their back on the restrictions of ordinary existence. They face in another direction. They stand in a magic circle, and their life is part of a magic ceremony, producing wonderful results (Key 19). Their daily experience is a verification of the principles of practical occultism (Key 14). Their inner life is a joyous union with the Higher Self. Nothing resists their will, because they have identified their "personal will" with the One Will behind the order of the Universe.

Note the significance of the verb, identified – *establish or indicate who or what (someone or something) is.* (Key 9). An adept gives visible signs of mastery because they have come into the realization that their true Self is the Eternal Master of All (Key 4).

In Chapter 3 of the *Bhagavad-Gita*, Krishna says: "There is nothing for me to do in these three worlds — nothing unattained that is possible to attain; still I am present in action."

The Supreme Self is the Doer of all. It is present in action, and the action is unceasing. The Self is eternally at rest in its Divine Perfection (Key 7). The cycles of manifestation follow each other in the continual flux of involution and evolution. However, the Self remains poised and unmoved, like the sphinx at the top of the wheel in Key 10.

Unceasing change of form necessitates the passing away of old forms so that new ones may come into manifestation. This is the framework of the Life-power's self-expression. In *The Book of Tokens*: "I am the germ; I am the growth; I am the decay." The Self remains unchanged amid change (Key 13)- only forms perish. There can never be permanence in form. The attempt to establish forms which shall be everlasting is the fundamental error, exemplified by the story of the Tower of Babel (Key 16).

Summary

The Intelligence of Desirous Quest and Key 10 is: The cyclic nature of manifestation shows an unbroken involution of spiritual potencies, balanced by a continuous evolution of manifested forms of expression. No structure can be final, because no form can terminate the manifestation of inexhaustible possibilities.

This is the idea expressed in Key 0, The Fool. No matter the height of self-expression the Life-power attains, there is always be a greater height beyond. To know this is to be free from two mistaken desires.

1. The desire to perpetuate some particular form;

2. The desire to attain some form of expression which is believed to be ultimate or final.

Liberation is not the attainment of changeless conditions. Freedom is nothing like that. It consists of spiritual knowing or conscious identification with THAT, which, though it enters into all forms, is restricted by none of them. The object of our desires is not a form at all, but the spiritual Reality behind all forms. We do not seek a final condition, because reason tells us there can be no such thing. Our quest is for identification with that which is beyond all bounds of name and form.

Our goal is Eternal Life. "And this is the way to have eternal life—to know you, the only true God, and Jesus the Christ, the one you sent to earth." – John 17:3.

MEDITATIONS

1st DAY: Keys 4, 13, 17, 7. The Universal Mind, comprehending all phenomena and their significance, is a real presence in my life. Daily I become more and more responsive to the influx of its wisdom. Established in right meditation, I see this day new forms of truth.

My personal life is the field of manifestation for the victorious spirit.

2nd DAY: Keys 15, 9, 10, 12. Every problem contains its answer. My true Self knows now whatever is hidden from my vision. Every situation in which I find myself is an aspect of the universal order.

This day I resign myself utterly to the unfailing support of the one reality.

3rd DAY: Keys 11, 13, 14, 8. All my actions are expressions of universal powers. Day by day, I am transformed into a more perfect likeness of my true Self. I am under guidance always.

My true self is now master of all conditions.

4th DAY: Keys 16, 6, 5, 19. Nothing in my life is, or can be, separated from the Universal Life. The real source of all my activities, conscious and subconscious, is a power flowing into the field of personality from the superconscious. As I listen and obey, the Inner Voice gives freely of its wise counsel.

This is a day of regeneration.

5th DAY: Keys 19, 14, 9, 4. My whole life is a ceremony, expressing the heavenly order. This day I verify the principles of true occultism. I identify my volition as being one with the Universal Will.

My true self is the eternal master of creation.

6th DAY: Keys 7, 10, 13, 16. The Supreme Self is present in all actions. It remains poised and firm amid change. Let forms pass: IT remains.

I am free from desire for the continuance of any form.

TAROT INTERPRETATION

Chapter 22

The 6th Stage of Spiritual Unfoldment – Realization

The Tarot Magic Square for this lesson is:

8	18	19	5
13	11	10	16
9	15	14	12
20	6	7	17

$8 + 18 + 19 + 5 = 50.$
$13 + 11 + 10 + 16 = 50.$
$9 + 15 + 14 + 12 = 50.$
$20 + 6 + 7 + 17 = 50.$

The sum of the numbers from 5 to 20 is 200.

The constant summation is 50. This indicates Key 5, the Hierophant considered as the operation of the power of Key 0, The Fool, through the agency of Key 5.

This tableau shows how the power of intuition (Key 5) formulates the energy of superconsciousness (Key 0). The tableau is related to the 16th Path of Vav (ו), the Eternal Intelligence. "The 16th Path is the pleasure (Eden) of the Glory. There is no Glory like it (beneath it). It is called the Garden of Eden prepared for the Merciful Ones (Saints)."

The message of the Inner Voice is the purest joy. The pleasure comes when our interior hearing enables us to identify the Self in us with that eternal I AM. Its essence is the AIN (אין) or No-Thing, which we call *All the power that ever was or will be.* The glory of that power is revealed to us, and the experience is the Hindus' "Existence-Knowledge-Bliss-Absolute."

This revelation of the Self includes the awareness of conscious immortality, symbolized by Key 20. To hear the Voice of the Eternal is to share its knowledge that the Self was never born and never dies. *Transcendental Magic, Its Dogma and Ritual* by Eliphas Levi, quotes a "16th Century manuscript" that lists the powers of the Hebrew letters (see Appendix). The power of Vav is, "Knows the reason of the past, present, and future." Past and present and future have their reason for existence, or their cause, in eternity. Eternity is always Now. When the Inner Voice speaks, the fact of eternity is a direct, present realization and is seen to be the cause of the illusion of time.

Three centers of the body are active when we hear the Inner Voice, the auditory center in the brain, the pituitary body or Moon center, and the Venus center in the throat. In medical astrology, Taurus rules the ears, jaw, and throat as an organ of speech. Venus rules Taurus and the place of the Moons exaltation.

$$5 - 19 - 18 - 8$$

By listening to the Inner Voice, the vibration of the three centers involved in interior hearing is activated. It is set up by energy originating in superconscious levels, instead of air-waves contacting on our eardrums. The physical organs of normal hearing are set in motion by etheric impulses, having their origin in the Universal Mind (Key 5). Interior hearing is facilitated by the conscious realization that sensations may be experienced, originating in our external physical environment.

The "inner sensorium," which gives us spiritual hearing, sight, and other spiritual sensations, is our normal senses stimulated by etheric impulses. With the mystery concerning the higher kinds of perception is dissipated, we direct our senses to be receptive toward the spiritual stimuli. This is represented by Key 19, and the two figures are shown as little children. When we begin this practice, we learn the significance of our inner sensations, just as children have to learn the meaning of ordinary sensations (Key 19).

By turning our attention to the inner life, we gradually organize these bodily centers that are used to contact the higher planes. The path is

210

shown in Key 18 leads to heights in the far background of the picture. The symbolism shows the goal of occult practice — the direct experience of the interior Reality and its power, which is the background of our external life. We cannot hear the Inner Voice unless we have ears to hear. Organic development is a necessary condition for spiritual experience Key 18.

This development is automatic when we grasp the principle involved and make that principle the basis of our practice of life. That is, subconsciousness is the bodybuilder. Subconsciousness is amenable to the dominant suggestion originating at the self-conscious level.

It is our thoughts, words, and deeds that formulate the idea that we are on the Path of Return. We are ripening into beings having ears to hear and eyes to see. The subconscious organizing power automatically takes care of the complex processes whereby the actual physiological readjustments are effected (Key 8).

The earlier stages of readjustment are similar to the process of erecting a new building on the site of an old one. First, the old building is torn down. Therefore, the serious undertake a life of regeneration, we invite and experience a period of mental, emotional, and physical upset. Many beginners believe they will be shining exceptions to this rule. Therefore, many enthusiastic aspirants abandon their practice. They lament their apparent misfortunes. In a vain effort to retain their cake while eating it, they fail miserably (Key 16).

Even this apparent failure is part of the ripening process. All of us have failed again and again, but our inability to remember past incarnations mercifully hides our failures behind a veil of forgetfulness. From these abortive attempts comes the impulse which drives us to seek release. Sooner or later, that impulse will be fully realized, and we shall complete our quest (Key 10).

The magical path requires faithful adherence to what we know and constant practice of the best type of life our present understanding shows us. The intermittent, casual effort gives little to no benefit. There must be daily, hourly, and momentary adjustments. The practice is continual vigilance, careful weighing of every motive and act, with determined elimination of mental, emotional, and physical state which holds us back. These are necessary to the unfoldment of the higher orders of knowing (Key 11).

The secret of the Great Work is dissolution, and dissolution and death are synonyms! Your old personality must be dissolved before the new personality can be formulated. Just as a caterpillar's body, inside its cocoon, loses all its characteristic parts before reforming, so does the occultist's mental concept of personality have to be dissolved before it may be reconstituted in the New Image (Key 13).

12 – 14 – 15 – 9

This dissolution is not the destruction of the physical body. It is the renunciation - the total renunciation and repudiation - of the conception of human personality held by the uninitiated or natural man. It is the reduction of that false notion to absolute nothingness until the seeker's consciousness retains no trace of affinity with the world's incorrect interpretation of the meaning of personality. This utter reversal of ordinary opinion is the true meaning of alchemical dissolution (Key 12).

They who regard every event of their life as being a particular dealing of God with their soul acts from motives different than those which are behind the ordinary person's thoughts and deeds. The psychological effect of this new point-of-view is significant. Only the ignorant believe that their powers are adequate to effect the work of regeneration. We must invoke the aid of a power higher than ourselves if we are to succeed in the Great Work.

Ageless Wisdom gives rational support to our faith, instead of the irrational acceptance of creeds and authority demanded by exoteric religion. Confidence we must have; because we cannot succeed without it. However, ours is a reasonable faith, susceptible to experimental verification (Key 14).

Our work demands a faith because the occultist is confronted early in their endeavors to escape from delusion, with many a vivid apparition of the Terrible. The Dweller on the Threshold is not a fanciful creation. The adoption of the magical path does not immediately remove problems from our way. On the contrary, our early experiences usually bring us face to face with a host of issues (Key 15).

Many experience loneliness. Many aspirants are abandoned by their friends and family because they find your motives incomprehensible.

However, freedom lies the severing of bonds; it hurts. It often seems that the aspirant is working without a glimmer of light from above. To all who are beset by such feelings, Ageless Wisdom says, "Whether you realize it or not, you are never alone. Always there stands the Silent Watcher, holding up the lamp of truth to light your way. Persist, and in due season you will reach the goal, the goal of absolute identification with that One. Attainment seems far removed from your present situation. That One is your true Self. Advance within the height where He stands (Key 9).

17 – 7 – 6 – 20

Meditation is the method for the work of readjustment. The practice of meditation brings about subtle psychological changes; among them are the balancing and coordination of the activities of the interior stars or chakras (Key 17). By meditation, one comes to know that personality is a vehicle for the real Self (Key 7). Meditation leads to correct discrimination and the balancing of the activities of the conscious and subconscious levels of personal action (Key 6).

Meditate on the idea of release from the time-bound, three-dimensional consciousness of uninitiated humanity into the conscious immortality and fourth-dimensional experience of the initiate (Key 20).

20 – 15 – 10 – 5

The *time* of that release, no one knows. They who ask, "How long will it take me to attain liberation?" betray their ignorance of fundamentals. Eliphas Levi says, *"The occultist must work as if he had all eternity to complete his undertaking."* The essence of occult attainment is unrelated to time as we understand time (Key 20).

The illusion of illusions is the appearance that we are not now what we shall one day become. The speed of those changes depends on elements we cannot possibly calculate. There have been instances in which the transformation of personalities appear to be instantaneous.

The main point is that the transformation is in the vehicle, not in the Self. You are, at this very moment, all that you aspire to become. The delusion that you are something else is the root error from which occult practice will release you (Key 15).

At the center of a wheel, there is no movement. At the core of your existence is the changeless Spirit of Life. When you have arrived at the goal, you discover that you were never anywhere else. It is a paradox. It is also a fundamental truth (Key 10).

Who is the Speaker whose Voice is heard in the Silence? Your Self. Who is the Knower from whose inexhaustible store of wisdom you may receive light on all your problems? It is your Self. To know the Self, to comprehend its exhaustless power, to express that power in every detail of personal existence, is the sum of occult attainment (Key 5).

8 – 11 – 14 – 17

You have come in touch with this work because you are ripening into the New Image. Whether you have any particular external evidence or not, the subtle power of the law which transforms personality is at work in you (Key 8).

Be faithful in the little things of daily practice, and you will find yourself entrusted with the adjustment of greater things (Key 11). YOU are among the called. You are among those whose lives are under the immediate supervision of Those Who Know. You are in the midst of a process of transmutation, which shall change all the base metal of your nature into pure gold (Key 14). Let this thought be the focal point of your meditations during the coming week, and be sure to make a note of any unveilings of truth which may come to you during this period (Key 17).

MEDITATIONS

1st Day: Keys 5, 19, 18, 8. Instructed by the *Inner Voice*, I turn away from the limitations of the outer senses, so that *my body may be transformed into the new image, through the unfailing strength of the perfect law.*

2nd Day: Keys 16, 10, 11, 13. Let every vestige of the false life be cleared away, that *through the right comprehension of the law, I may be faithful in even the least things, thus dissolving every trace of the error of separateness.*

3rd Day: Keys 12, 14, 15, 9. Daily I reverse the false concepts of the world, submitting every detail of my life to the guidance of the *True Self,* facing every problem courageously, and *relying confidently on the power of the Silent Watcher.*

4th Day: Keys 17, 7, 6, 20. I will persist in meditation until I realize fully the Indwelling Presence of the One Self, and *experience that perfect balance of my inner powers, which shall release me from Time into Eternity.*

5th Day: Keys 20, 15, 10, 5. I am not in haste, for I know all adversity shall be overcome in due season if I but *listen to the inner Voice and obey its admonitions.*

6th Day: Keys 8, 11, 14, 17. The perfect Law works in my flesh to eliminate all embodiments of delusion and balance all forces, to the end *that I may enjoy the Knowledge and Conversation of the Guardian Angel, and witness the Unveiled Truth.*

Tarot Interpretations

Chapter 23

The 7th Stage of Spiritual Unfoldment – Cosmic Consciousness

The Tarot Magic Square for this lesson is,

9	19	20	6
14	12	11	17
10	16	15	13
21	7	8	18

$9 + 19 + 20 + 6 \quad = 54.$
$14 + 12 + 11 + 17 = 54.$
$10 + 16 + 15 + 13 = 54.$
$21 + 7 + 8 + 18 \quad = 54.$

The sum of the numbers from 6 to 21 is 216.

The constant summation is 54. This indicates Key 9, The Hermit, is the operation of the power symbolized by Key 4, The Emperor, working through the agency represented in Tarot by Key 5, The Hierophant.

The Hermit corresponds to the 20th Path on the Tree of Life, Intelligence of Will. The Sepher Yetzirah says: "The 20th Path is the Intelligence of Will. It is the trait from which everything is formed. Through this consciousness, everyone can know the essence of the Original Wisdom."

Will in Hebrew is רצון, *Rawson*. The four letters correspond to the four elements.

Letter		Element
Resh	ר	Fire or radiant energy
Tzaddi	צ	Air
Vav	ו	Earth
Final Nun	ן	Water

The significance of the word relates to the idea of a synthesis of the four elements, which is the One Reality, the Ancient of Days represented by the Hermit, and designated by the Divine Name IHVH (יהוה) – Jehovah.

In the "Mind of the Father" (*Chaldean Oracles*), are the primary patterns of all things. Each pattern is a mental embodiment of the intention or purpose, or Will, of the Universal Mind. These archetypal patterns are maintained throughout a cycle of manifestation and imposed upon all centers of life-expression.

These patterns in the mind of the Father are the conditions of manifested existence, the archetypal roots of all states of embodiment. Orderly formulation of knowledge concerning these conditions is the method of exoteric and esoteric science.

Exoteric science considers our environment as forces or conditions external to humanity. Occult science declares that the Mind of the Father is a real presence in every human being. ''The Father and I are One,'' Jesus said. It is a fact even for those who do not realize it.

Occult Science declares that the power which forms the patterns of OUR bodies is an integral part of our constitution. It follows that the conditions around us are not imposed from outside, but are expressions of our innermost Will.

To know the will of the Father requires the understanding of the differences between the functions of the conscious and subconscious minds. Among the most potent causes of our predicaments is attempts to do consciously what ought to be done subconsciously and the subconscious attempting self-conscious activities, like reasoning.

The conscious mind is the watcher and initiator of action. Subconsciousness is the body-builder and the link between personality and the Universal Self. *All practical occultism is a development of the fundamental facts and laws illustrated by Key 6.*

6 – 20 – 19 – 9

The sum of the numbers from 1 to 6 is 21 (1 + 2 + 3 + 4 + 5 + 6 = 21). This is equivalent to saying that what is represented by Key 21 is the unfoldment of the possibilities shown in Key 6.

This week's tableau reminds us that to know the Will of the Father. We use the law of suggestion to turn the subconscious mind, like a mirror, so that it reflects the light of super-consciousness into the field of personality (Key 6). Conscious immortality is the consequence of our subconscious contact with the true Self. For when that contact is established, the body-building functions of subconsciousness are modified. The patterns in the Universal Mind are reflected into our personality. There follows a reorganization of the personal vehicle. This reorganization includes the awakening of the functions of specific bodily centers, which enable us to become consciously aware that we are four-dimensional eternal beings (Key 20).

This regeneration is physical and mental (Key 19). The regenerative process turns us away from the limitations of the senses and opens to us the glories of the supersensual realm. In this realm, we establish contact with the Intelligence of Will and realize at last our identity with the Silent Watcher (Key 9).

The truth about the Self unveils during our hours of meditation. As it is written in Light on the Path: "Look for the flower to bloom in the silence that follows the storm, not till then." Key 17 symbolizes meditation. Therefore it is placed immediately after the one which shows a violent storm (Key 16). Only through right meditation can confidence be developed in the absolute justice of cosmic law. Such confidence is indispensable to them who would establish equilibrium in their personality (Key 11). It is because the practice of meditation puts us in touch with the Inner Life that it is insisted upon in all manuals of practical occultism. Again we quote from Light on the Path, ''Within you is the light of the world. Through your own heart comes the one light which can illuminate life and make it clear to your eyes."

These quotations are from the portions numbered 12 in the first and second sections of Light on the Path. They correspond with the Hanged Man (Key 12). After the suspension of personal action and the resignation of the individual life to the guidance of Universal Spirit, comes the Knowledge and Conversation of the Holy Guardian Angel. That Angel effects the transmutation of all the base elements of personal life (Key 14).

13 – 15 – 16 – 10

The ardent desire for power is required of us, but the power we are taught to desire is not power over others. It is in contact with the Life-power, and this contact is often described as "knowledge." But this is not superficial brain knowledge. It is an intimate union, approximating the Biblical "to know" and the sublimation of the forces corresponding to Scorpio (Key 13). The knowledge brings about the development of the inner senses and the understanding of the significance of the mixtures of elemental forces.

To the outer eye, these elemental combinations seem chaotic. Their activities seem to be opposition to our plans and purposes. To the spiritual eye, they present another aspect. When that eye is opened, the Adversary is recognized as a friend, wearing a mask of terror while He teaches us how to play the game of life (Key 15).

Through his instruction, we learn to conquer the false desires and are enabled to overthrow our errors erected on separateness (Key 16). Ultimately we discover the truth that everything in our environment is related to everything else. We see our existence as part of the cycle of manifestation. We perceive that the events of today are connected with the past and joined with the future (Key 10).

Following the Path of Return, which leads within, we pass beyond the limits of ordinary experience into that vast Beyond. From here come the reports of Those Who Know, our Elder Brothers and Sisters who have preceded us. We are on the same path as They, for all that they seem so far beyond us.

From them comes the message: The whole nature of humanity must be used wisely by the one who desires to enter the way. For occult development is not complete until the outermost vehicle of Spirit, the physical body, has been transformed by the renewal of the mind (Key 18). In this transformation, the work is almost all subconscious. The conscious mind perceives the law and formulates the demand or pattern. The actual reorganization which brings the animal nature under control is effected at subconscious levels (Key 8). Hence, "Kill out the hunger for growth." The transformation which is to be effected is not growth, not the addition of somewhat we do not possess. Instead, is it a rearrangement of the vehicles of consciousness into better coordination or alignment. The Self is all that we aspire to be – an infinitely more. Not attainment, in the ordinary sense of the word, but realization is the Goal (Key 7). No words can describe the realization. It is conscious identification with Universal Spirit. Perfect peace, perfect bliss, perfect knowledge. All this it is, and more than this (Key 21).

21 – 16 – 11 – 6

The Administrative Intelligence, which corresponds to the final Tarot
Key, means "the Serving Intelligence." Cosmic consciousness, or
identification with the Universal Spirit, finds expression of the
heavenly order here on earth. They who know the truth need to live it.
Thenceforth they are a servant of the ALL. Not as a duty hard to carry
out, but as a natural expression of our place in the cosmic order (Key
21). For such a person, selfish personal aims are automatically at an
end (Key 16). They look at their life as a manifestation of adjustments
that maintains the cosmic equilibrium. They manifest Karma or work.
Since their will is aligned with the Universal Will, their actions are
effective (Key 11). They act as a witness of the universal order. They
know that alert watchfulness is necessary. They are intent on each
succeeding phase of experience. Most of all, their intent is a reception
from the superconscious Will through the channel of
subconsciousness (Key 6).

The conscious mind, by right reasoning, infers the presence of the Universal Will as the guiding power. Even though the Silent Watcher be unseen, correct reasoning shows that He is present (Key 9). It follows that the logical procedure is to submit the whole personal life to that Higher Guidance.

By repeated self-reminder, one comes to regard all operations of the personal life as having their source in super-sensual and super-personal planes of the Life-power's activity (Key 12).

This intellectual correction of appearances does not banish the appearances, during ordinary states of waking consciousness. The illusion of separateness continues, but the delusion which accepts this illusion as reality is overcome (Key 15). Eventually, every cell of the body is influenced by the change in mental attitude. Through the processes of physical elimination, the old physical body, conceived in ignorance, ceases to exist and is replaced by a new body.

This is a physical body in certain respects different enough that it can be considered a new species. These are the bodies of adepts and Masters. Human in form, but superhuman in their capacity for utilizing and transforming rates of vibration which would disintegrate the ordinary human vehicle (Key 18).

MEDITATIONS

1st DAY: Keys 6, 20, 19, 9. Subconsciousness reflects the light and wisdom of the Oversoul into my field of personal awareness. Therefore I receive the power of eternal life amid this illusion of temporal existence.

I am beginning to live the life of regeneration. I know my identity with the Silent Watcher.

2nd DAY: Keys 17, 11, 12, 14. The flower of realization blooms in the silence of meditation. I am sure of the absolute justice of cosmic law. The light of the world is within me.

That light transmutes my whole existence into its likeness.

3rd DAY: Keys 13, 15, 16, 10. Even the least of my activities is a transformation of the One Life-power. Thus I know that whatever mask of terror confronts me is veiling the face of the Eternal Friend. All semblances of stress and terror are but preludes to the dawn of the Great Peace.

This day the Wheel of Life turns forward for my good.

4th DAY: Keys 18, 8, 7, 21. I follow the Path of Return, transforming my body by the renewal of my mind. My life today is a stage in my progress toward the perfect demonstration of the Great Secret. My true Self is, even now, all that I aspire to be.

I am all peace, all bliss, and all knowledge.

5th DAY: Keys 21, 16, 11, 6. Let me be a servant of all. No aim is mine that others cannot share. I am an instrument of the Life-power's perfect ability to adjust all things for good.

Let me be intent on the perception of the Great Purpose.

6th DAY: Keys 9, 12, 15, 18. Though I see Him not, I feel today the presence of the Silent Watcher. I submit my whole life to His perfect guidance. Thus I recognize every appearance of separateness and chaos as being a veil of illusion, and I am not deluded by these surface appearances.

Even in my flesh, I shall see God.

TAROT INTERPRETATION

Chapter 24

Tarot Key Permutations

The 22 Tarot Keys may be combined to form 112 groups of nine Keys, each group containing nine cards, numbered consecutively. This does not include the various magic square arrangements, such as we have been using in this course.

The Keys in every group follow a natural order. The 112 combinations fall into eight classes. Inspection of the tables will show that in each set of fourteen groups, the first arrangement of nine Keys sets the pattern for all other groups of that class. No two arrangements are the same. Every one conveys its distinct shade of meaning.

FIRST CLASS

0	1	2
3	4	5
6	7	8

1	2	3
4	5	6
7	8	9

2	3	4
5	6	7
8	9	10

3	4	5
5	6	8
9	10	11

4	5	6
7	8	9
10	11	12

5	6	7
8	9	10
11	12	13

6	7	8
9	10	11
12	13	14

7	8	9
10	11	12
13	14	15

8	9	10
11	12	13
14	15	16

9	10	11
12	13	14
15	16	17

10	11	12
13	14	15
16	17	18

11	12	13
14	15	16
17	18	19

12	13	14
15	16	17
18	19	20

13	14	15
16	17	18
19	20	21

SECOND CLASS

2	1	0
5	4	3
8	7	6

3	2	1
6	5	4
9	8	7

4	3	2
7	6	5
10	9	8

5	4	3
8	7	6
11	10	9

6	5	4
9	8	7
12	11	10

7	6	5
10	9	8
13	12	11

8	7	6
11	10	9
14	13	12

9	8	7
12	11	10
15	14	13

10	9	8
13	12	11
16	15	14

11	10	9
14	13	12
17	16	15

12	11	10
15	14	13
18	17	16

13	12	11
16	15	14
19	18	17

14	13	12
17	16	15
20	19	18

15	14	13
18	17	16
21	20	19

THIRD CLASS

0	3	6
1	4	7
2	5	8

1	4	7
2	5	8
3	6	9

2	5	8
3	6	9
4	7	10

3	6	9
4	7	10
5	8	11

4	7	10
5	8	11
6	9	12

5	8	11
6	9	12
7	10	13

6	9	12
7	10	13
8	11	14

7	10	13
8	11	14
9	12	15

8	11	14
9	12	15
10	13	16

9	12	15
10	13	16
11	14	17

10	13	16
11	14	17
12	15	18

11	14	17
12	15	18
13	16	19

12	15	18
13	16	19
14	17	20

13	16	19
14	17	20
15	18	21

FOURTH CLASS

6	3	0
7	4	1
8	5	2

7	4	1
8	5	2
9	6	3

8	5	2
9	6	3
10	7	4

9	6	3
10	7	4
11	8	5

10	7	4
11	8	5
12	9	6

11	8	5
12	9	6
13	10	7

12	9	6
13	10	7
14	11	8

13	10	7
14	11	8
15	12	9

14	11	8
15	12	9
16	13	10

15	12	9
16	13	10
17	14	11

16	13	10
17	14	11
18	15	12

17	14	11
18	15	12
19	16	13

18	15	12
19	16	13
20	17	14

19	16	13
20	17	14
21	18	15

FIFTH CLASS

6	7	8
3	4	5
0	1	2

7	8	9
4	5	6
1	2	3

8	9	10
5	6	7
2	3	4

9	10	11
6	7	8
3	4	5

10	11	12
7	8	9
4	5	6

11	12	13
8	9	10
5	6	7

12	13	14
9	10	11
6	7	8

13	14	15
10	11	12
7	8	9

14	15	16
11	12	13
8	9	10

15	16	17
12	13	14
9	10	11

16	17	18
13	14	15
10	11	12

17	18	19
14	15	16
11	12	13

18	19	20
15	16	17
12	13	14

19	20	21
16	17	18
13	14	15

8	7	6
5	4	3
2	1	0

9	8	7
6	5	4
3	2	1

10	9	8
7	6	5
4	3	2

11	10	9
8	7	6
5	4	3

12	11	10
9	8	7
6	5	4

13	12	11
10	9	8
7	6	5

14	13	12
11	10	9
8	7	6

15	14	13
12	11	10
9	8	7

16	15	14
13	12	11
10	9	8

17	16	15
14	13	12
11	10	9

18	17	16
15	14	13
12	11	10

19	18	17
16	15	14
13	12	11

20	19	18
17	16	15
14	13	12

21	20	19
18	17	16
15	14	13

SEVENTH

8	5	2	9	6	3	10	7	4
7	4	1	8	5	2	9	6	3
6	3	0	7	4	1	8	5	2

11	8	5	12	9	6	13	10	7
10	7	4	11	8	5	12	9	6
9	6	3	10	7	4	11	8	5

14	11	8	15	12	9	16	13	10
13	10	7	14	11	8	15	12	9
12	9	6	13	10	7	14	11	8

17	14	11	18	15	12	19	16	13
16	13	10	17	14	11	18	15	12
15	12	9	16	13	10	17	14	11

20	17	14	21	18	15
19	16	13	20	17	14
18	15	12	19	16	13

2	5	8	3	6	9	4	7	10
1	4	7	2	5	8	3	6	9
0	3	6	1	4	7	2	5	8

5	8	11	6	9	12	7	10	13
4	7	10	5	8	11	6	9	12
3	6	9	4	7	10	5	8	11

8	11	14	9	12	15	10	13	16
7	10	13	8	11	14	9	12	15
6	9	12	7	10	13	8	11	14

11	14	17	12	15	18	13	16	19
10	13	16	11	14	17	12	15	18
9	12	15	10	13	16	11	14	17

14	17	20	15	18	21
13	16	19	14	17	20
12	15	18	13	16	19

There are fourteen groups in each class. You can use two every day for eight weeks. Set up one tableau of nine Keys for your morning meditation, and the next one just before going to bed. Try to write out, from these tableaus, groups of meditations similar to those you have received in this course.

Until you have tried this for yourself will you discover that Tarot evokes what is in our minds, rather than putting something into them. Do not let the uninteresting appearance of the tables keep you from making full use of them.

When you write your meditations, use the first suggestion which comes to you. Sometimes it will be a bit of the symbolism which will start your train of thought. At other times, the Hebrew letter, or some of its attributions, will provoke a response. If you have worked with the Cube of Space in *Tarot Fundamentals*, that will bring much to you.

You will never exhaust the possibilities of Tarot. There are no less than 1,124,727,777,607, 680,000 different permutations of the 22 major. No two combinations mean precisely the same.

Since the Tarot is almost infinite in its combinations, there are innumerable ways to use it. Up to now, the emphasis has been on yourself. These courses intend to teach you the fundamental knowledge required for you to practice intelligent self-direction.

The wisdom of Tarot is the art of directing the cosmic forces which surround and play through you. Tarot has to do with the relationships between your personality and other humans constituting the social order in which you live.

Before one may hope to understand others, you must know yourself. Before one may serve or direct others, we must have established some degree of self-command.

If you worked persistently and faithfully with the lessons, your personality is different from the one who opened the first lesson. New vistas have shown themselves to you. Ideas that may have been difficult at first are now easier to grasp. Changes have been made in your mentality, and transformations have been effected in the chemistry of your body. You are now ready to render a wider service to humanity.

In the last lesson in *Tarot Interpretation*, you will be given additional instruction in the concrete application of the Tarot to living the awakened life.

TAROT INTERPRETATION

Chapter 25

Epilogue and Test

This final lesson is intended to point out various ways to use the combinations of Tarot Keys, apart from their employment in exercises in meditation.

Suppose you have a specific problem. Consider it carefully. Then, it will be relatively easy to determine what Key symbolizes the essential nature of the problem. Then select one of the tableaus or magic squares in which that Key is a central unit. Lay this arrangement of Keys before you, and look at it, with the definite intention of letting it evoke from your inner consciousness a suggestion of what should be your next step.

Do not try to force an answer. Sit ten or fifteen minutes, with a pencil and paper at hand for notes of any ideas which may come to you. If none comes at the first sitting, do not be discouraged. Sometimes these hints from within come during the day, after the morning practice with the Keys. Often they pop into your head just as you are waking the next morning. However, this may work out, be sure to follow the suggestion.

Another use of the squares and tableaus is to give you a better understanding of your individuality and personality. To learn more about your individuality, use the squares and tableaus in which the central unit is the key corresponding to your *Sun sign*. To learn more about your personality, use the squares and tableaus in which the central unit is the Key representing your *rising sign*; also, those in which the central unit is the Moon sign in your natal chart. If you do not know your Rising or Moon sign, consult an astrologer.

By using the same method, you can better understand the lives of persons with whom you are associated. Even those who puzzle or annoy, you may be less of a mystery if you use the Tarot to help you get below the surface of their outward behavior.

239

You may also use these combinations of Keys to developing a better knowledge of the particular principles and laws concerning the realization of your heart's desire. What you want to be and do, more than anything else, is an expression symbolized by a Tarot Keys. *It may take time to determine which Key stands for what you want, but you will find it if you look.*

Even solid objects are embodiments of seed ideas in the Universal Mind. Tarot is a catalog of the fundamental seed ideas and their relations to one another. Therefore you may use the Tarot to help you develop clear images to express what you wish to experience.

What Jung calls the "collective unconscious" is a vast reservoir of seed ideas. They are held in the collective unconscious as symbols. The Chaldean Oracles say: "The Father of gods and men placed the mind (nous) in the soul (psyche), and placed both in the (human) body. The Paternal Mind has sown symbols in the soul. The symbols in the collective unconscious are the seeds of all possible combinations of physical conditions that may be experienced by humanity.

To be able to evoke the images which correspond to the conditions we desire to have manifested in our environment is to possess a key to power. We do not break the web of Maya or illusion by trying to destroy Maya. What liberates us is the right use of the symbols sown in the soul. These seed ideas are the basis of our environment. The entire structure of the physical universe is made up of some ninety-two combinations of protons.

The combination of protons is called an element. For example, Hydrogen has one proton. Helium has two protons, etc. Therefore, the complexity of the universe is the expression of a relatively small number of principles, which are the basis of everything in our experience.

Furthermore, physical manifestation is the consequence of the creative mental activity of the Originating Spirit. That Spirit is omnipresent and is therefore present in humanity. Today, as always, it creates with the thought process. From our self-conscious human point of view, it appears that the physical universe, its energies, and laws were here before humans appeared on the scene. They will remain after we leave.

Ageless Wisdom agrees, but the truth goes farther. As an individual, we had nothing to do with our appearance on Earth. As an individual, we do not set the stage. But within our personality dwells a higher life, which is the real Being assuming the outward mask of the personal existence.

This Being, the true I AM within us, is the only God there is. This is the inner significance of Exodus 3:14, where God tells Moses his name, ehyeh ašer ehyeh (אהיה אשר אהיה), *I am who I Am, or I will be what I will be, or I create whatever I create*. Therefore the Bible tells us that the true "God" is the Absolute Being – I AM.

Ageless Wisdom says the true Self at the center of every personality is identical with the Originating Spirit. Identical with it, not derived from it. Personality is a derivative. The Self is ONE.

Fortunately, we do not have to grasp the full meaning to use the power it gives us. We act as if it were true. This is the basis of theurgy, or God-working, as contrasted with various forms of sorcery, which aim to bolster up the weakness of human personality by calling outside entities to its aid.

Much which passes for religion is a form of sorcery. When prayer is conceived as being a method whereby the person praying flatters or compels, some being outside to fulfill our desires, that prayer is a form of false magic. When prayer is recognition of an indwelling power, able to modify external conditions because it is the power that brings to pass every external manifestation, this is sincere prayer or theurgy.

Various New Thought groups glimpse at this truth. Their methods are correct, but it is limited by a misunderstanding of the law. The law or practice is focusing on creative seed ideas in subconsciousness. This is the law at work in our use of the Tarot.

Humanities' place in the cosmic order is to act as a distributor for the power of the Originating Spirit. Humans can bring into concrete manifestation new combinations of the seed ideas in Universal Mind. By doing so, we "control" the forces of our environment, and brings into tangible existence, conditions that would never make their appearance except for the action of human self-consciousness.

Humans do not exert personal control of circumstance, even when we can perform works of power which seem like miracles. Theurgy is based on a recognition we do nothing. We do not control. We act as conscious instruments of the original Creative Power, which operates through us —in harmony with its immutable laws. When we are awakened from the dream of separateness, we know the indwelling presence of this Creative Power and are made aware of its laws of manifestation. Then we obey the laws, and the results amaze those who do not share the wisdom which comes from within and above.

The beginning of the modification of our environment was probably the domestication of wild animals, by subjecting their lower order of intelligence to human directions. Then came agriculture, establishing conditions in which grass was transformed into grain. Step by step, man's consciousness was fashioned by the Life-power, and through combinations of energy known as tools (every mechanism invented by humans is an adaptation of invisible powers. These powers are our mental interpretation of sensations calls "things," are various forms of electromagnetic energy), humans extended the empire of self-consciousness over subconsciousness. So was developed tools whereby the forces in our environment are made to serve us.

Human personality is the most excellent tool of all, like other tools, may be improved. Human character continually expresses the Administrative Intelligence symbolized by Tarot Key 21. When one realizes this, it becomes a perfect human personality.

By perfect, we do not mean that personality is to be brought to absolute perfection. What we mean is that the average human does not live up to the true standard of personality. The evolutionary process brings our personality to a "diamond in the rough." Even the more "advanced" races (as their members like to imagine) are not perfect instruments for the Life-power's self-expression. Furthermore, members of supposedly "backward" races may and do, equal and sometimes surpass, the achievements of members of races, which were supposed to be the "flower of humanity."

There are no superior and no inferior races. Superior personalities predominate over inferior ones in every race. We have to learn the lesson of Key 14. Wherever a superior personality appears, that person knows that they were fashioned by the Life-power. This is one of the distinguishing characteristics of every truly superior man or woman.

Before this, higher self-knowledge blossoms into full splendor, a preparatory period, during which one seems to be in the midst of sharp conflict. We appear to make intense personal effort precedes the actual realization. Mere lip-service to the idea that the Life-power is the only Thinker and the only Actor is not enough. The wise agree that even the perfected personality, except in rare moments of ecstasy, remains in the illusion of separateness. Consequently, we must exert what seems to be "our" will, but all our exertion consists in the effort to surrender our will to the One Will. In the external affairs of human existence, these people are active, diligent, and hardworking.

These individuals experience the same illusion as the rest of humanity. However, they are never deluded by them. Thus their whole motivation is different, and so is their primary purpose.

Such a perfected human personality knows the beautiful truth about the destiny of humanity. We are sons and daughters of God, "There is no God but Man," the Rosicrucians say. In every human's innermost being is the essential Reality that we call "God."

Human personality masks our true nature. This mask makes unenlightened human beings appear to one another like animals or objects. This delusion is characteristic of the majority in incarnation. Some have escaped from this delusion. To them, we owe the Ageless

Wisdom, which tells us we are destined to become true sons and daughters of the Most High. We are instruments whereby divine powers manifest in our environment and human society.

The power which condensed the physical objects is present in us all. It works from the center outward. The laws are summarized in the Tarot. Tarot is one of several symbols of the Creative Pattern. We may follow this pattern to produce selected results. Using Tarot in this way, we establish in our field of personal subconsciousness the seed ideas, which are the universal basis for the forms we desire to see around us. This is theurgy.

There is no intrinsic power in a Tarot Key. It is not Tarot that works. A Tarot Key is a pictorial symbol of a principle or law of life. It influences subconsciousness because the natural language of the collective subconsciousness is graphic imagery. While you hold the image of a Key in your consciousness, your subconsciousness is being impressed with the meaning of that image.

Day after day, week after week, your attention is focused on combinations of Tarot symbols. This work may seem mechanical and boring at times. Seed-planting is not exciting. But, if you have stuck to your practice, you have impressed your subconsciousness with the fundamental principles of the universal creative process.

By using many different combinations of Keys, you avoided the danger of specializing on those that you fancied, while neglecting others. This course provides you with daily exercises in the employment of the subtle power suggested by the images.

Tarot Interpretation Test

1. Give three examples of meditations based on the Tarot Keys, as explained in the previous lesson.

2. What is your understanding of the term, "Magic of Light"?

3. Name the seven stages of spiritual unfoldment.

[Paul Case doesn't list the seven stages in these lessons. They are found in Tarot Fundamentals. See Appendix 1 for a summary.]

Appendix 1 – The Seven Stages of Spiritual Unfoldment

Stage 1: Key 15 – Bondage

Will-power is cosmic energy, not a personal force. So long as humans suffer from the delusion that they possess wills of their own, they remain in bondage. To think of Willpower as one's personal property or attribute is absurd. One might as well claim to own the air one breathes.

Key 15, the Devil, depicts a man in woman in bondage. But this is an illusion based on superficial appearances. The gross, repellant surface of this Key represents the illusion. You must see through the illusion to find Key 15's real meaning.

Stage 2: Key 16 – Awakening

The flash of spiritual illumination overthrows false structures of wrong thought and action;

Key 16 is the second stage of spiritual unfoldment. It is the awakening from the nightmare of bondage. The first stage, represented by Key 15, is the realization of the nature of bondage; that is, ignorance. And when we understand the truth, the lighting flash illuminates the darkness, and the bad dream is over.

Key 16 is a picture of destruction, but the source of the destructive power is the Sun. The disintegrating force comes forth like a streak of lightning. It refers to the flash of superconsciousness, which constitutes the first awakening.

Stage 3: Key 17 – Meditation/Revelation

Then comes a period of quiet like the calm, which follows a storm. During this quiet, new relations come to us through meditation.

The third stage of spiritual unfoldment is *Revelation*. Revelation is *unveiling, disclosure, and discovery*. The seeker does not make the discovery. It is made to them. We receive the revelation. We do not lift the veil of Isis. She unveils herself.

Thus Key 17 pictures an operation above the level of personal human consciousness. The physical senses do not perceive disclosures made at this stage. They are not conclusions reached by the reasoning mind, based on observing externals – quite the reverse. These revelations come when the reasoning mind is wholly stilled and the senses sealed.

Stage 4: Key 18 – Organization

The term *organization,* as used here, means the organization of the various parts of the human body into a higher type of organism than that are not spontaneously provided by evolution.

Stage 5: Key 19 – Regeneration

The fifth stage of spiritual unfoldment is symbolized by Key 19, which is the new birth from natural humanity into spiritual humanity. Every ceremonial presentation of the process of regeneration employs this symbolism of rebirth.

Stage 6: Key 20 – Realization

Key 20 shows the sixth stage of spiritual unfoldment, in which the personal consciousness is verging of blending with the universal. At this stage, the adept realizes that their existence is nothing but a manifestation of the relation between self-consciousness and subconsciousness. The adept sees that self-consciousness and subconsciousness are modes of universal consciousness. The adept knows their personality has no separate existence. At the 6th stage, the intellectual conviction is *confirmed by a fourth-dimensional experience*, which blots out the delusion of separateness.

Stage 5: Key 21 – Cosmic Consciousness

The last card of the major Tarot Keys is *The World*. It is symbolic of the 7th stage of spiritual unfoldment, cosmic consciousness, or Nirvana. The identification with the One Power which is the Pivot and Source of the whole cosmos. The adept at this stage experience firsthand through their personality the Power, which governs and directs the universe flows out into manifestation. This is always true. But experiencing such a thing is another matter.

Words fail to express the seventh stage of spiritual unfoldment. It is left to your intuition combined with the suggestions of the picture with the meaning of Tav (ת). Key 21 is a picture of what you are, and of what the cosmos is. The universe is the Dance of Life. The innermost, Central Self of *your personality* is the Eternal Dancer. It always has been; it always will be.

Appendix 2

The Powers of the Hebrew Letters

Transcendental Magic, Its Dogma and Ritual by Eliphas Levi,

There is indeed a formidable secret, the revelation of which has already transformed the world, as testified in Egyptian religious tradition, symbolically summarized by Moses at the beginning of Genesis. This secret constitutes the fatal science of good and evil, and of its revelation is death. Moses depicts it once consequence under the figure of a tree which is in the center of the Terrestrial Paradise, is in proximity to the tree of life and has a radical connection therewith; at the foot of this tree is the source of the four mysterious rivers; it is guarded by the sword of fire and by the four figures of the Biblical sphinx, the Cherubim of Ezekiel. Here I must and I fear... pause, already that I have said too much. Yes, there is one sole, universal, and imperishable dogma, strong as the supreme reason; all that like all that is simple, like is great; intelligible, universally and absolutely true; and this dogma has been the all others. Yes, there is a science which parent of confers on man powers apparently superhuman; I find them enumerated as follows in a Hebrew manuscript of the sixteenth century:

"Hereinafter follow the powers and privileges of him who holds in his right hand the Clavicles of Solomon, and in his left the Branch of the Blossoming Almond."

Aleph (א). He beholds God face to face, without dying, and converses familiarly with the seven genii who command the entire celestial army.

Beth (ב). He is above all afflictions and all fears.

Ghimel (ג). He reigns with all heaven and is served by all hell.

Daleth (ד). He rules his own health and life and can influence equally those of others.

He (ה). He can neither be surprised by misfortune, nor overwhelmed by disasters, nor conquered by his enemies.

Vau (ו). He knows the reason of the past, present, and future.

Zain (ז). He possesses the secret of the resurrection of the dead and the key of immortality.

Such are seven chief privileges, and those which rank next are these:

Cheth (ח). To find the philosophical stone.

Teth (ט). To possess the universal medicine.

Yod (י). To know the laws of perpetual motion and prove the quadrature of the circle.

Kaph (כ). To change into gold not only all metals, but also the earth itself, and even the refuse of the even the earth

Lamed (ל). To subdue the most ferocious animals and have the power to pronounce words which paralyze and charm serpents.

Mem (מ). To have the Ars Notoria which gives the universal science.

Nun (נ). To speak learnedly on all subjects, without preparation and without study.

These, finally, are the seven least powers of the Magus.

Samek (ס). To know at a glance the deep things of the souls of men and the mysteries of the hearts of women.

Gnain (ע). To force nature to make him free at his pleasure.

Phe (פ). To foresee all future events which do not depend on a superior free will, or on an undiscernible cause.

Tsade (צ). To give at once and to all the most efficacious consolations and the most wholesome counsels.

Koph (ק). To triumph over adversities.

Resh (ר). To conquer love and hate.

Shin (ש). To have the secret of wealth, to be always its master and never its slave. To know how to enjoy even poverty and never become abject or miserable.

Tau (ת). Let us add to these three septenaries that the wise man rules the elements, stills the tempests, cures by diseased his touch, and raises the dead!

But certain things have been sealed by Solomon with his triple seal. It is enough that the initiates know, as for others, whether they deride, doubt or believe, whether they threaten or fear, what matters it to science or to us?"

Appendix 3 – Phi and the Pentagram

The Divine Proportion is also called the Golden Mean, Golden Section, Golden Cut or the phi (ɸ) ratio.

Expressed mathematically the phi ratio is,

When solving this equation we find that the roots are

$$\phi = \frac{1 + \sqrt{}\sqrt{5}}{2} \sim 1.618... \quad \text{or} \quad \phi = \frac{1 - \sqrt{5}}{2} \sim -0.618...$$

~ Means approximately equal to

Phi is an irrational number so it does not have an exact decimal value, just better and better approximations.

For more information of the math properties of phi, I recommend the YouTube channel, Numberphile.

The Pentagram

The five pointed star cannot be drawn exactly with a compass and straight edge. However, in AutoCAD, it can be drawn to 16 decimal points of accuracy. This precision allows the analyses of the pentagram to be taken to the next level.

Consider a circle with Radius = 1 with an inscribed pentagram.

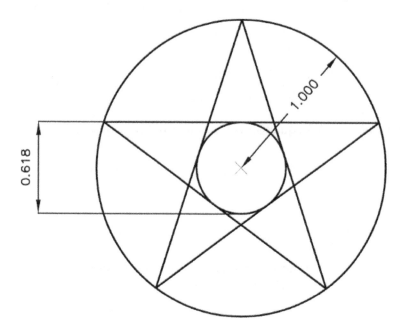

Notice the ratio of the outer circle to the inner circle is.

$$\frac{1.000}{0.618} = 1.618$$

Note that $1/\phi = 0.618$

The pentagrams can be nested and the phi ratio is continuously expressed by the ratio of the circles.

To show the next expression of phi, I scaled up the figure to make phi easier to see.

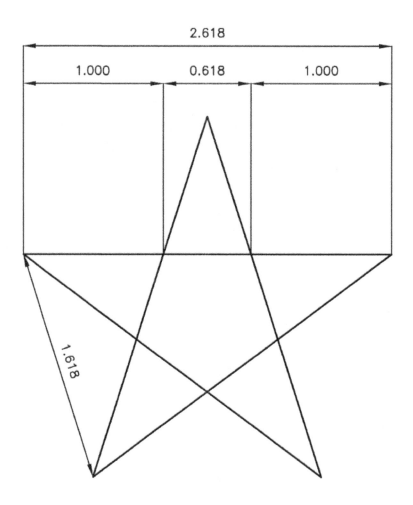

I was aware that the length of the line that describes a pentagram contains the phi ratio. I was pleasantly surprised to see the distance between the points of the pentagram are also phi.

Summary

What does this mean?

A pentagram is a symbol of humanity the microcosm and God the macrocosm. The four lower points of the pentagram a symbol of the four elements with the top point representing spirit and reason.

The phi ratio being expressed the idea that the part encodes the whole. This is consistent with the holographic universe.

Appendix 4 – Squaring the Circle

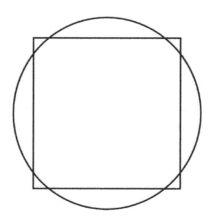

In esoteric thought, squaring the circle is the question, how does matter (square) related to spirit (circle). This is shown by finding the circumference of a circle equal the perimeter of a square. With math and geometry the problem is easy to solve.

Squaring the Circle with Algebra

Start with a circle with Radius = 1.

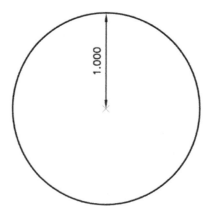

The circumference of a circle is the Diameter multiplied by Pi (π). The Diameter is twice the Radius.

$$D = 2R$$

$$\text{Circumference} = 2\pi R$$

With the radius = 1, Circumference = 2π

Pi is an irrational number (a number that cannot be precisely defined) whose approximate value is 3.1416.

Now to find a square with the same perimeter.

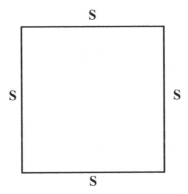

In a square, all sides are equal, therefore the perimeter of a square is 4 times the length of a side.

Perimeter = 4S

Then we set the **Circumference** of the Circle equal to the **Perimeter** of the square.

$$\text{Circumference} = 2\Pi R$$

$$\text{Perimeter} = 4S$$

Therefore, $4S = 2\Pi R$

With R = 1, the equation is $4S = 2\Pi \, \pi$

To solve for S (side) we divide both sides of the equation by 4.

$$S = \frac{2\Pi}{4}$$

Or S = Π/2,

Π = 3.14159265…

S = 1.5708

And easy as pie, the problem is solved. However, Pi is an irrational number with no exact value, so how do you draw the squaring of the circle?

Squaring the Circle with Geometry

The Great Pyramid Giza

To solve the squaring the circle geometrically, we need the third dimension.

Consider a circle with Radius = 1. Then the Height of the pyramid is 1. The perimeter of the base is 2Π and the length of each side is π Π / 2.

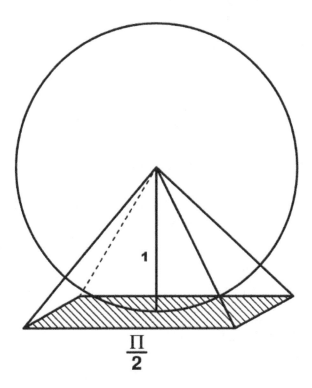

$$\frac{\Pi}{2}$$

Note that triangle that forms the face of the pyramid is tilted approximately 32 degrees toward the center of the pyramid.

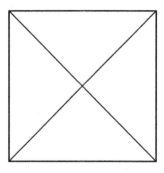

Top View of Pyramid

Then the only question that remains is, what does the triangle that makes up the pyramid look like?

We know that the height of the triangle is 1 and the base is $\pi \Pi / 2$.

The elevation view (side view) of the triangles that form the pyramid we can see some interesting properties.

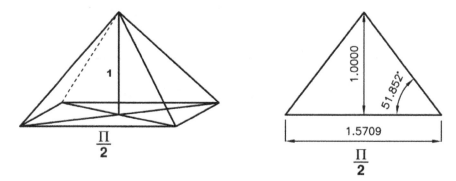

As seen from this perspective, the angel of the triangle is 51.85°, which is very close the Great Pyramid in Gaza Egypt – 51.84°.

From another perspective, we can see another interesting relationship.

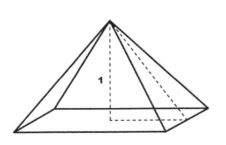
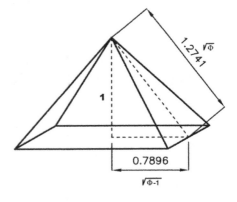

Let's examine the interior triangle more detail.

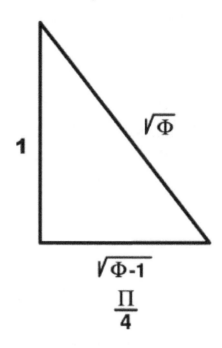

$$\frac{\Pi}{4}$$

An interesting relationship can be seen.

$\pi \, \Pi \, / \, 4 = 0.7854$

Square Root $(\phi - 1) = 0.7861$

Conclusion

The circle represents spirit, the square matter. These are two dimensional figures. To square the circle requires a third dimension that is less than a one percent the shape of the Great Pyramid of Giza. Inherent in the geometry of the pyramid is the number *Phi* and *Pi*. Thus the combination of the square (matter) with the circle (spirit) is life (*Phi*). This is a representation of The Living Stone or the Stone of the Wise.

Appendix 5

The Most Perfect Fractal

I have a curious mind that leads me all over the place, like fractals.

A **fractal** is a natural phenomenon or a mathematical set that exhibits a repeating pattern that displays at every scale. It is also known as **expanding symmetry** or **evolving symmetry**. If the replication is the same at every scale, it is called a self-similar pattern. - Wikipedia.

The simplest three-dimensional figure is a triangle. But which triangle?

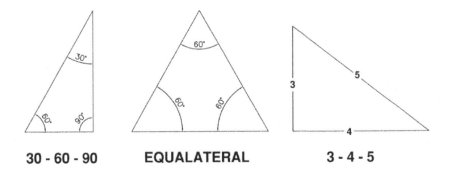

30 - 60 - 90   **EQUALATERAL**   **3 - 4 - 5**

The equilateral is the simplest and most elegant to work with. Then, to create a fractal, triangles are nested inside each other.

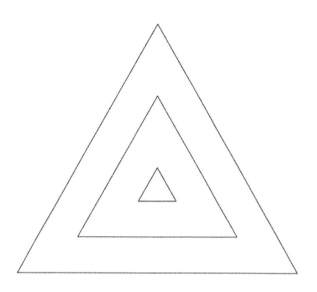

For the example above, I choose an arbitrary nesting of triangles.
However, what is the most beautiful or perfect spacing of triangles?

My Favorite Numbers

I keep a list of my favorite numbers on a corkboard.

Number	Value		Number	Value
Π (pi)	3.1416		√2	1.4142
Φ (phi)	1.618		1/√2	0.7071
1/Φ	0.618		√3	1.7321
Φ²	2.618		1/√3	0.5774
			√5	2.2361
e	2.718		1/√5	0.4472
e^{Π}	23.140			
Π^e	22.459		√2/√3	0.816
α	1/137		√3/√2	1.225
α = fine structure			√2/√5	0.633
constant			√3/√5	0.775
			√5/√3	1.291
			√5/√2	1.581

I choose the natural log to the base e.

Limit $(1 + 1/n)^n = 2.718...$
$n \to \infty$

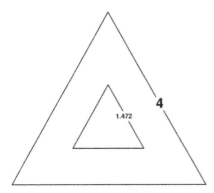 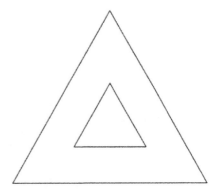

The ratio of sides of the two triangles is close to the value of e (Because e is irrational, and does not have a precise amount).

The spacing didn't look quite right. Then I noticed that e is very close to the value of

$1 + \sqrt{\sqrt{3}} = 2.732$

I compared the two triangles.

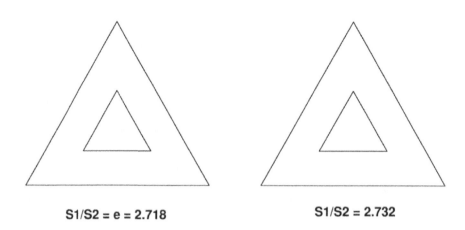

S1/S2 = e = 2.718   S1/S2 = 2.732

It's difficult to see the difference. However, on a big screen, the nested triangles on the right are more pleasing to the eye.

Of course, this solution left me with more questions than it answered.

Why does the nesting triangles on the right more pleasing? How can I construct these figures with a compass and straight edge?

That's when things get a little hazy. One night I felt inspired and made a drawing, printed it out, and put it in my inbox. Other projects took my time, and I didn't get back to this project for several weeks.

A few weeks later, after a meditational shower, I get inspired to finish the project. I look through my inbox and find a single sheet of paper with this drawing.

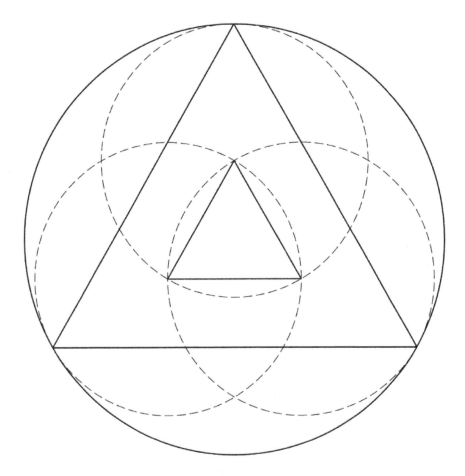

Handwritten on the paper was this equation:

$$R_1 = R_2(1 + 1/\sqrt{}\sqrt{3})$$

R_1 = Radius of outer circle
R_2 = Radius of inner circle

I look closely at the paper. Yup, that's my handwriting, alright. But how did I arrive at the equation? I look through my desk, and this is the only documentation. Now I am getting worried as my wet hair drips on drawing because I have no idea how I arrived at the equation.

I smile, realizing that I have just manifested a reoccurring dream. I am showing up naked to a math test.

I get on the computer and check my AutoCAD files. Just the same drawing with different colored lines and circles. Then I remember, the construction lines were interfering with the beauty and symmetry of the drawing. So I erased everything and zoomed in to admire the perfect triangles inside the perfect circles. Then I shut down the computer confident that everything I needed to know contained in the drawing and equation.

So I turn on AutoCAD and do some reverse engineering.

R_1 is the Radius of the outer circle.

R_2 is the Radius of the three inner circles.

Figure 1 – Draw a Circle with Triangle

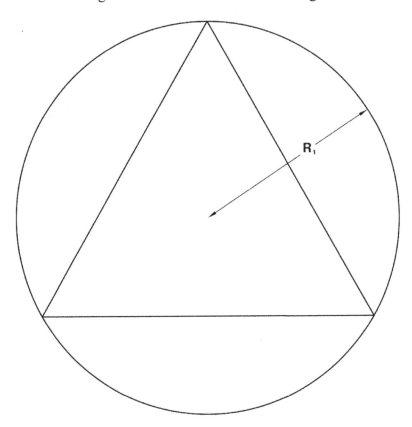

Figure 2

Draw 3 circles of R_2

Since $R_1 = R_2(1+1/\sqrt{}\sqrt{3})$

Then

$$R_2 = \frac{R_1}{(1+1/\sqrt{}\sqrt{3})}$$

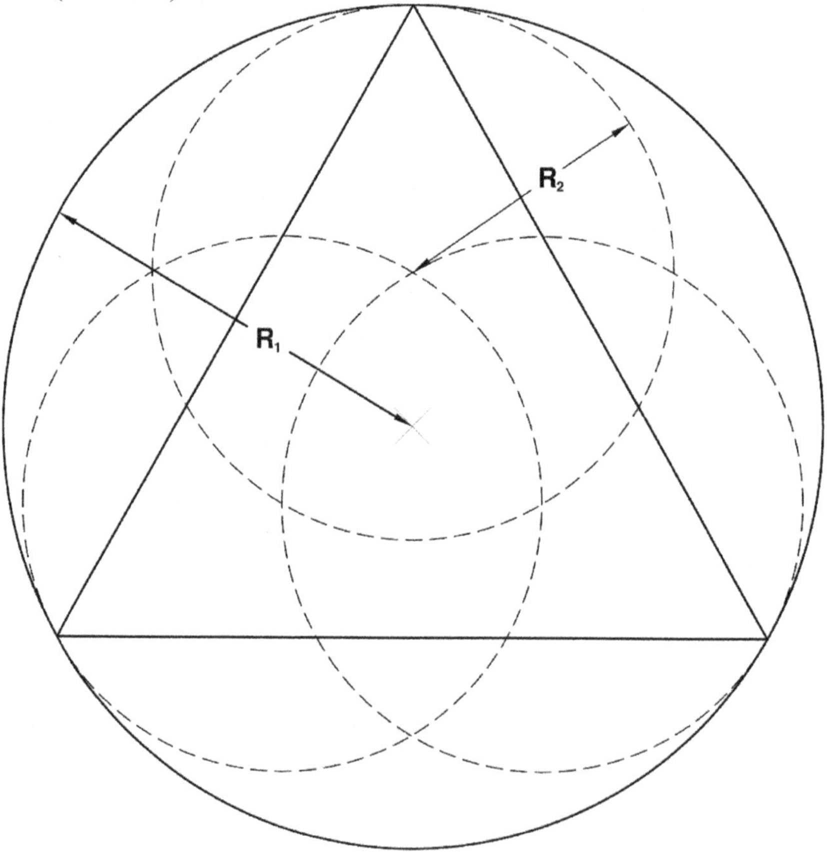

$R_1 = 6.309$ $R_2 = 4$

$$R_1 = R_2\left(1+\frac{1}{\sqrt{3}}\right)$$ $$R_2 = \frac{R_1}{\left(1+\dfrac{1}{\sqrt{3}}\right)}$$

Figure 3

Draw Interior Triangle

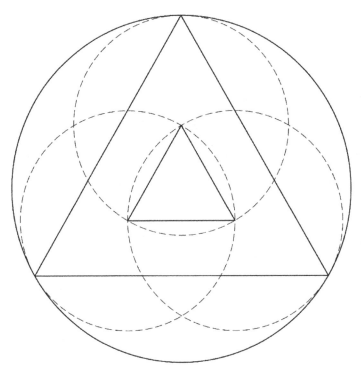

In three easy steps, I recreated my original drawing. However, the answer left me with more questions.

1. Why is this arrangement of triangles pleasing to the eye?

2. Why does the math work out?

So I made more measurements.

Figure 4

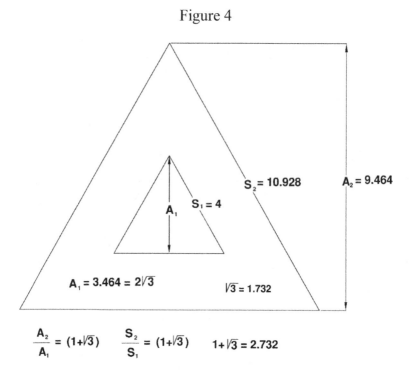

$$\frac{A_2}{A_1} = (1+\sqrt{3}) \qquad \frac{S_2}{S_1} = (1+\sqrt{3}) \qquad 1+\sqrt{3} = 2.732$$

Notice that both the sides and the altitude or height of the triangle are related to 1 plus the square root of three.

Figure 5

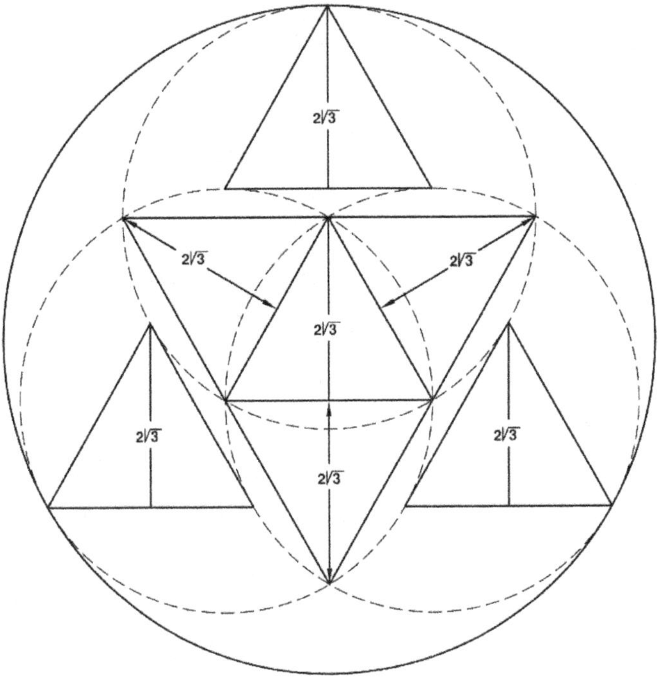

The figure also inscribes seven identical triangles.

Figure 6

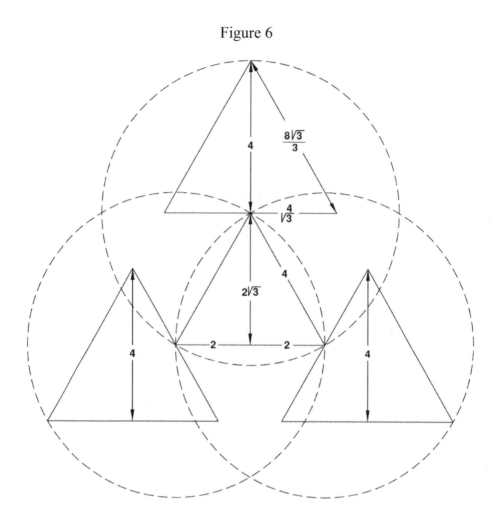

By shifting the sides of the triangles, so they touch, the side of the central triangle is equal to the altitude or height of the outer triangles.

Figure 7

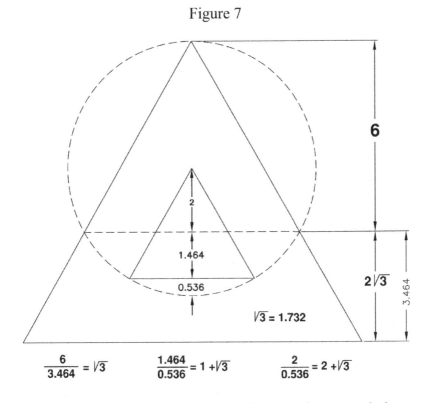

$$\frac{6}{3.464} = \sqrt{3} \qquad \frac{1.464}{0.536} = 1 + \sqrt{3} \qquad \frac{2}{0.536} = 2 + \sqrt{3}$$

Dividing the triangles as shown above, also reveals more relations to the square root of three.

277

Figure 8

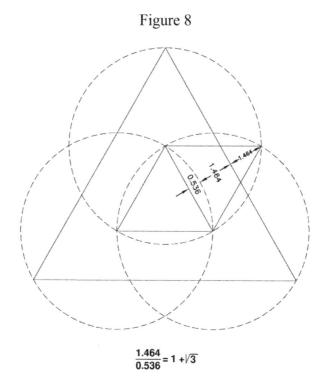

$$\frac{1.464}{0.536} = 1 + \sqrt{3}$$

From another perspective, the square root of three shows up again.

Figure 9

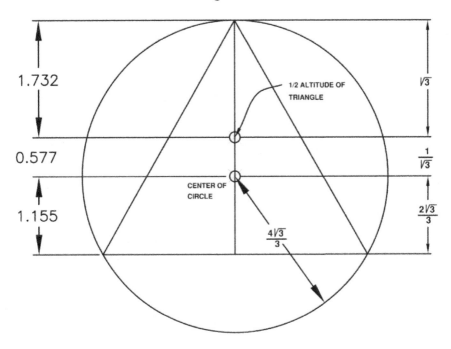

If we zoom in on the central triangle, things get interesting. Recall from Figure 2 that,

$$R_1 = R_2\,(1+1/\sqrt{3})$$

Notice the $1/\sqrt{3}$ that's the distance between the center of the circle and one half the altitude of the triangle.

I've already led you down a long rabbit hole, but this drawing deserves more explanation.

Figure 10

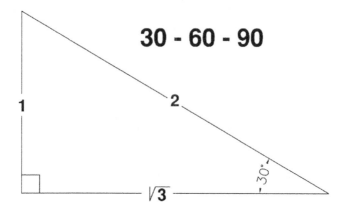

30 - 60 - 90

This figure explains the next three figures. If you not into geometry, you can stop here. But for those who want to proof, enjoy.

Figure 11

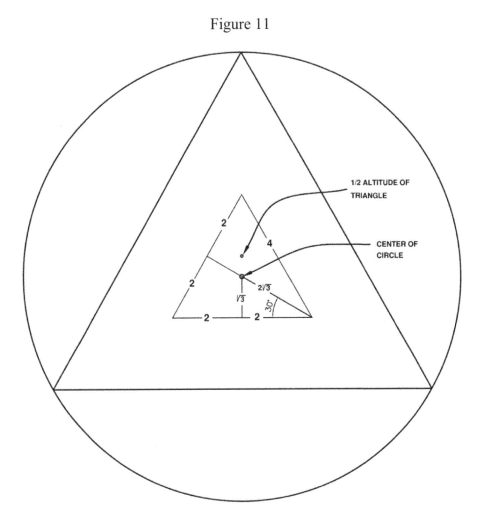

Figure 12

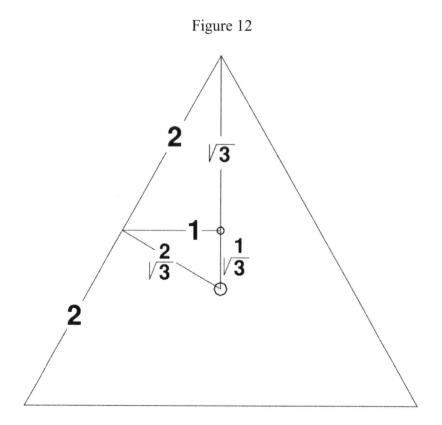

Figure 13

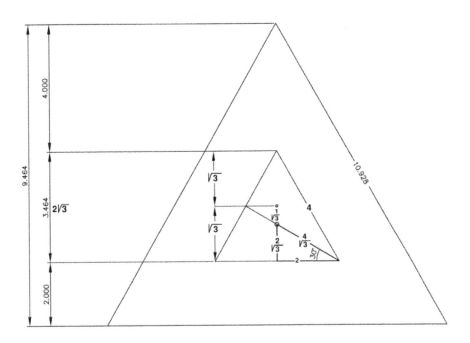

Why is this the Perfect Fractal?

All these beautiful and symmetrical arrangements break down when you deviate from this equation.

$$R_1 = R_2(1+1/\sqrt{}\sqrt{3})$$

The only way to vary the ratio of the triangles is to vary the ratio of the circles. When I did, the symmetry disappeared. For example, instead of using the square root of three, I used the square root of 4, which is 2.

Figure 14

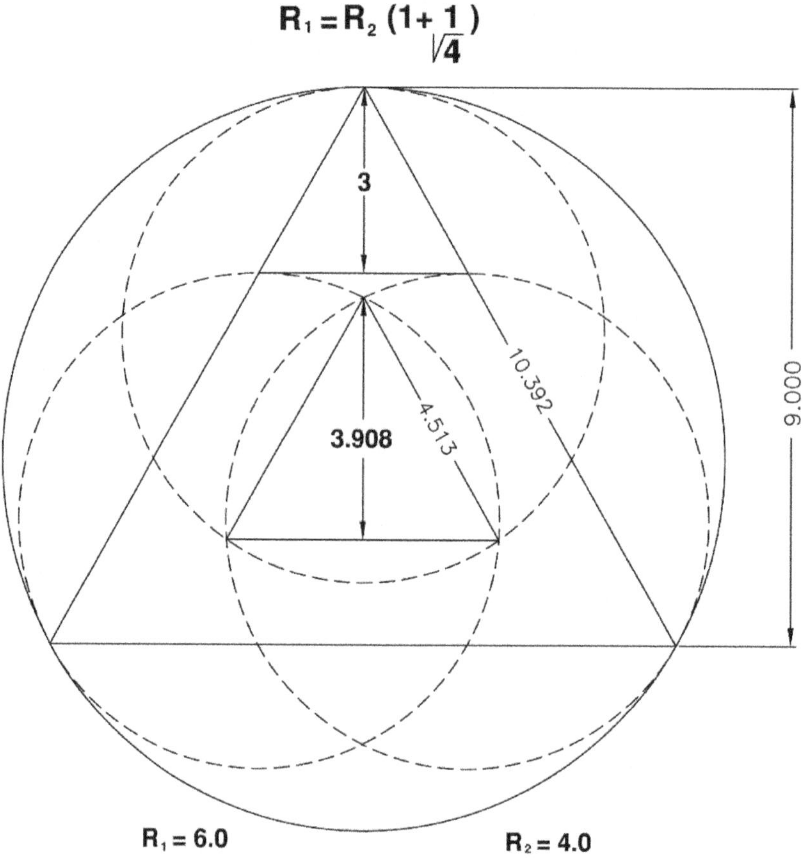

$$R_1 = R_2 \left(1 + \frac{1}{\sqrt{4}}\right)$$

$R_1 = 6.0$ $R_2 = 4.0$

Then I compared the drawing to the square root of three.

Figure 15

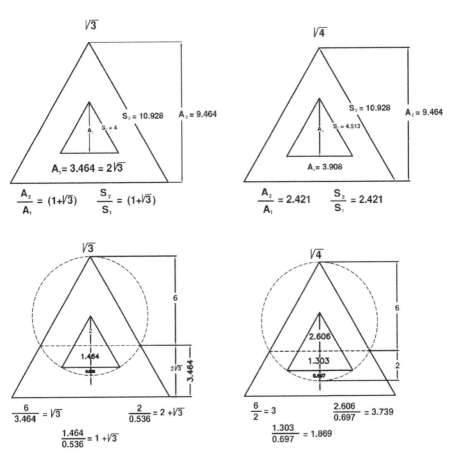

Notice that the ratios of the square root of 4 do not have elegant solutions.

Then I compared the drawing to the square root of two.

Figure 16

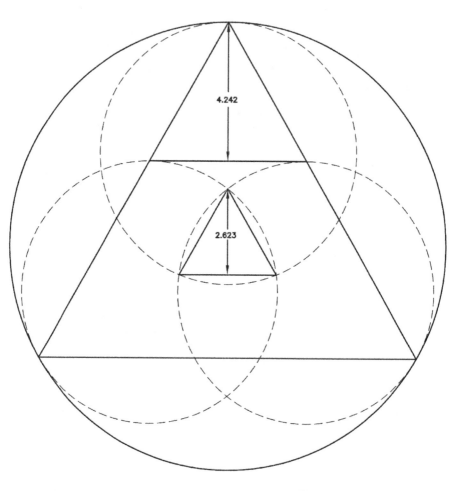

$$R_1 = R_2 \left(1 + \frac{1}{\sqrt{2}}\right)$$

$R_1 = 6.828$

$R_2 = 4.0$

Figure 17

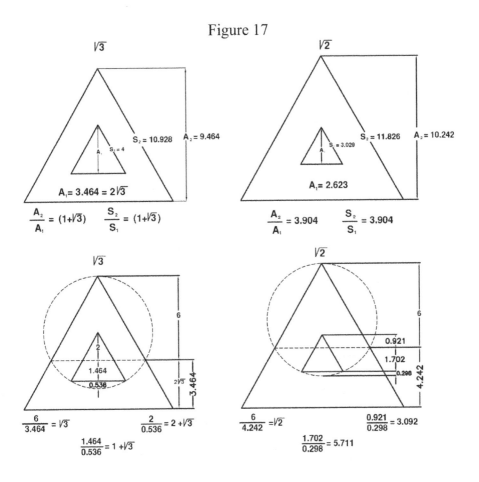

Notice also the square root of 2 doesn't have a beautiful solution.

Conclusion

The *symmetry exists, IF and ONLY IF* $R_1 = R_2(1+1/\sqrt{3})$.

287

Made in the USA
Coppell, TX
17 February 2021